On
Communication
(Vol. 2)

HBR's 10 Must Reads series is the definitive collection of ideas and best practices for aspiring and experienced leaders alike. These books offer essential reading selected from the pages of *Harvard Business Review* on topics critical to the success of every manager.

Titles include:

HBR's 10 Must Reads 2015
HBR's 10 Must Reads 2016
HBR's 10 Must Reads 2017
HBR's 10 Must Reads 2018
HBR's 10 Must Reads 2019
HBR's 10 Must Reads 2020
HBR's 10 Must Reads 2021
HBR's 10 Must Reads for CEOs
HBR's 10 Must Reads for New Managers
HBR's 10 Must Reads on AI, Analytics, and the New Machine Age
HBR's 10 Must Reads on Boards
HBR's 10 Must Reads on Building a Great Culture
HBR's 10 Must Reads on Business Model Innovation
HBR's 10 Must Reads on Career Resilience
HBR's 10 Must Reads on Change Management (Volumes 1 and 2)
HBR's 10 Must Reads on Collaboration
HBR's 10 Must Reads on Communication (Volumes 1 and 2)
HBR's 10 Must Reads on Creativity
HBR's 10 Must Reads on Design Thinking
HBR's 10 Must Reads on Diversity
HBR's 10 Must Reads on Emotional Intelligence
HBR's 10 Must Reads on Entrepreneurship and Startups
HBR's 10 Must Reads on Innovation
HBR's 10 Must Reads on Leadership (Volumes 1 and 2)
HBR's 10 Must Reads on Leadership for Healthcare
HBR's 10 Must Reads on Leadership Lessons from Sports
HBR's 10 Must Reads on Lifelong Learning

HBR's 10 Must Reads on Making Smart Decisions
HBR's 10 Must Reads on Managing Across Cultures
HBR's 10 Must Reads on Managing in a Downturn, Expanded
   Edition
HBR's 10 Must Reads on Managing People (Volumes 1 and 2)
HBR's 10 Must Reads on Managing Risk
HBR's 10 Must Reads on Managing Yourself (Volumes 1 and 2)
HBR's 10 Must Reads on Mental Toughness
HBR's 10 Must Reads on Negotiation
HBR's 10 Must Reads on Nonprofits and the Social Sectors
HBR's 10 Must Reads on Organizational Resilience
HBR's 10 Must Reads on Platforms and Ecosystems
HBR's 10 Must Reads on Public Speaking and Presenting
HBR's 10 Must Reads on Reinventing HR
HBR's 10 Must Reads on Sales
HBR's 10 Must Reads on Strategic Marketing
HBR's 10 Must Reads on Strategy (Volumes 1 and 2)
HBR's 10 Must Reads on Strategy for Healthcare
HBR's 10 Must Reads on Teams
HBR's 10 Must Reads on Women and Leadership
HBR's 10 Must Reads: The Essentials

On
Communication
(Vol. 2)

HARVARD BUSINESS REVIEW PRESS
Boston, Massachusetts

MIX
Paper | Supporting responsible forestry
FSC™ C016779

ISBN: 978-1-64782-095-4
eISBN: 978-1-64782-096-1

Contents

On
Communication
(Vol. 2)

Leadership Is a Conversation

by Boris Groysberg and Michael Slind

THE COMMAND-AND-CONTROL APPROACH to management has in recent years become less and less viable. Globalization, new technologies, and changes in how companies create value and interact with customers have sharply reduced the efficacy of a purely directive, top-down model of leadership. What will take the place of that model? Part of the answer lies in how leaders manage communication within their organizations—that is, how they handle the flow of information to, from, and among their employees. Traditional corporate communication must give way to a process that is more dynamic and more sophisticated. Most important, that process must be *conversational*.

We arrived at that conclusion while conducting a recent research project that focused on the state of organizational communication in the 21st century. Over more than two years we interviewed professional communicators as well as top leaders at a variety of organizations—large and small, blue chip and start-up, for-profit and nonprofit, U.S. and international. To date we have spoken with nearly 150 people at more than 100 companies. Both implicitly and explicitly, participants in our research mentioned their efforts to "have a conversation" with their people or their ambition to "advance the conversation" within their companies. Building upon the insights and examples gleaned from this research, we have developed a model of leadership that we call "organizational conversation."

Elements of organizational conversation

Intimacy	Interactivity	Inclusion	Intentionality
How leaders relate to employees	*How leaders use communication channels*	*How leaders develop organizational content*	*How leaders convey strategy*
OLD MODEL: CORPORATE COMMUNICATION			
Information flow is primarily top-down	Messages are broadcast to employees	Top executives create and control messaging	Communication is fragmented, reactive, and ad hoc
Tone is formal and corporate	Print newsletters, memos, and speeches predominate	Employees are passive consumers of information	Leaders use assertion to achieve strategic alignment
NEW MODEL: ORGANIZATIONAL COMMUNICATION			
Communication is personal and direct	Leaders talk with employees, not to them	Leaders relinquish a measure of control over content	A clear agenda informs all communication
Leaders value trust and authenticity	Organizational culture fosters back-and-forth, face-to-face interaction	Employees actively participate in organizational messaging	Leaders carefully explain the agenda to employees
			Strategy emerges from a cross-organizational conversation
WHAT IT MEANS FOR EMPLOYERS AND EMPLOYEES			
Leaders emphasize listening to employees rather than just speaking to them	Leaders use video and social media tools to facilitate two-way communication	Leaders involve employees in telling the company story	Leaders build their messaging around company strategy
Employees engage in a bottom-up exchange of ideas	Employees interact with colleagues through blogs and discussion forums	Employees act as brand ambassadors and thought leaders	Employees take part in creating strategy via specially designed communication vehicles

Idea in Brief

One-way, top-down communication between leaders and their employees is no longer useful or even realistic.

Today's leaders achieve far more engagement and credibility when they take part in genuine conversation with the people who work for and with them. A conversation is a frank exchange of ideas and information with an implicit or explicit agenda.

Corporate conversation reflects a new reality: Thanks in part to digital and social technologies, employees have found a public voice. They'll use it whether their bosses like it or not.

The good news for leaders is that people can talk up a company in a way that's more interesting and attractive than any obvious public relations campaign.

Smart leaders today, we have found, engage with employees in a way that resembles an ordinary person-to-person conversation more than it does a series of commands from on high. Furthermore, they initiate practices and foster cultural norms that instill a conversational sensibility throughout their organizations. Chief among the benefits of this approach is that it allows a large or growing company to function like a small one. By talking with employees, rather than simply issuing orders, leaders can retain or recapture some of the qualities—operational flexibility, high levels of employee engagement, tight strategic alignment— that enable start-ups to outperform better-established rivals.

In developing our model, we have identified four elements of organizational conversation that reflect the essential attributes of interpersonal conversation: intimacy, interactivity, inclusion, and intentionality. Leaders who power their organizations through conversation-based practices need not (so to speak) dot all four of these i's. However, as we've discovered in our research, these elements tend to reinforce one another. In the end, they coalesce to form a single integrated process.

Intimacy: Getting Close

Personal conversation flourishes to the degree that the participants stay close to each other, figuratively as well as literally. Organizational conversation, similarly, requires leaders to minimize the

3

distances—institutional, attitudinal, and sometimes spatial—that typically separate them from their employees. Where conversational intimacy prevails, those with decision-making authority seek and earn the trust (and hence the careful attention) of those who work under that authority. They do so by cultivating the art of listening to people at all levels of the organization and by learning to speak with employees directly and authentically. Physical proximity between leaders and employees isn't always feasible. Nor is it essential. What *is* essential is mental or emotional proximity. Conversationally adept leaders step down from their corporate perches and then step up to the challenge of communicating personally and transparently with their people.

This intimacy distinguishes organizational conversation from long-standard forms of corporate communication. It shifts the focus from a top-down distribution of information to a bottom-up exchange of ideas. It's less corporate in tone and more casual. And it's less about issuing and taking orders than about asking and answering questions.

Conversational intimacy can become manifest in various ways—among them gaining trust, listening well, and getting personal.

Gaining trust.
Where there is no trust, there can be no intimacy. For all practical purposes, the reverse is true as well. No one will dive into a heart-felt exchange of views with someone who seems to have a hidden agenda or a hostile manner, and any discussion that does unfold between two people will be rewarding and substantive only to the extent that each person can take the other at face value.

But trust is hard to achieve. In organizations it has become especially difficult for employees to put trust in their leaders, who will earn it only if they are authentic and straightforward. That may mean addressing topics that feel off-limits, such as sensitive financial data.

Athenahealth, a medical-records technology provider, has gone as far as to treat every last one of its employees as an "insider" under the strict legal meaning of the term. Insiders are defined as employees entrusted with strategic and financial information that could materially affect the company's business prospects and hence its stock price—a status typically accorded only to top-tier officers. Opening the books to such a degree was a risky move, discouraged by the company's underwriters and frowned upon by the SEC. But Athenahealth's leaders wanted employees to become insiders in more than just the regulatory sense; they wanted them to be thoroughly involved in the business.

Listening well.

Leaders who take organizational conversation seriously know when to stop talking and start listening. Few behaviors enhance conversational intimacy as much as attending to what people say. True attentiveness signals respect for people of all ranks and roles, a sense of curiosity, and even a degree of humility.

Duke Energy's president and CEO, James E. Rogers, instituted a series of what he called "listening sessions" when he was the CEO and chairman of Cinergy (which later merged with Duke). Meeting with groups of 90 to 100 managers in three-hour sessions, he invited participants to raise any pressing issues. Through these discussions he gleaned information that might otherwise have escaped his attention. At one session, for example, he heard from a group of supervisors about a problem related to uneven compensation. "You know how long it would have taken for that to bubble up in the organization?" he asks. Having heard directly from those affected by the problem, he could instruct his HR department to find a solution right away.

Getting personal.

Rogers not only invited people to raise concerns about the company but also solicited feedback on his own performance. He asked employees at one session to grade him on a scale of A to F. The results, recorded anonymously, immediately appeared on a screen for all to see. The grades were generally good, but less than half of employees were willing to give him an A. He took the feedback seriously and began to conduct the exercise regularly. He also began asking open-ended questions about his performance. Somewhat ironically, he found that "internal communication" was the area in which the highest number of participants believed he had room for improvement. Even as Rogers sought to get close to employees by way of organizational conversation, a fifth of his people were urging him to get closer still. True listening involves taking the bad with the good, absorbing criticism even when it is direct and personal—and even when those delivering it work for you.

At Exelon, an energy provider headquartered in Chicago, a deeply personal form of organizational conversation emerged from a project aimed at bringing the company's corporate values alive for its employees. Values statements typically do little to instill intimacy; they're generally dismissed as just talk. So Exelon experimented in its communication about diversity, a core value: It used a series of short video clips—no fuss, no pretense, no high production values—of top leaders speaking unscripted, very personally, about what diversity meant to them. They talked about race, sexual orientation, and other issues that rarely go on the table in a corporation. Ian McLean, then an Exelon finance executive, spoke of growing up in Manchester, England, the son of a working-class family, and feeling the sting of class prejudice. Responding to a question about a time when he felt "different," he described going to work in a bank where most of his colleagues had upper-class backgrounds: "My accent was different. . . . I wasn't included, I wasn't invited, and I was made to think I wasn't quite as smart as they were. . . . I never want anyone else to feel that [way] around me." Such unadorned stories make a strong impression on employees.

Interactivity: Promoting Dialogue

A personal conversation, by definition, involves an exchange of comments and questions between two or more people. The sound of one person talking is not, obviously, a conversation. The same applies to organizational conversation, in which leaders talk *with* employees and not just *to* them. This interactivity makes the conversation open and fluid rather than closed and directive. It entails shunning the simplicity of monologue and embracing

The New Realities of Leadership Communication

FIVE LONG-TERM BUSINESS TRENDS are forcing the shift from corporate communication to organizational conversation.

Economic Change

As service industries have become more economically significant than manufacturing industries, and as knowledge work has supplanted other kinds of labor, the need for sophisticated ways to process and share information has grown more acute.

Organizational Change

As companies have become flatter and less hierarchical, and frontline employees more pivotally involved in value-creating work, lateral and bottom-up communication has achieved the importance of top-down communication.

Global Change

As workforces have become more diverse and more widely dispersed, navigating across cultural and geographic lines has required interactions that are fluid and complex.

Generational Change

As millennials and other younger workers have gained a foothold in organizations, they have expected peers and authority figures alike to communicate with them in a dynamic, two-way fashion.

Technological Change

As digital networks have made instant connectivity a norm of business life, and as social media platforms have grown more powerful and more ubiquitous, a reliance on older, less conversational channels of communication has ceased to be tenable.

---

the unpredictable vitality of dialogue. The pursuit of interactivity reinforces, and builds upon, intimacy: Efforts to close gaps between employees and their leaders will founder if employees don't have both the tools and the institutional support they need to speak up and (where appropriate) talk back.

7

In part, a shift toward greater interactivity reflects a shift in the use of communication channels. For decades, technology made it difficult or impossible to support interaction within organizations of any appreciable size. The media that companies used to achieve scale and efficiency in their communications—print and broadcast, in particular—operated in one direction only. But new channels have disrupted that one-way structure. Social technology gives leaders and their employees the ability to invest an organizational setting with the style and spirit of personal conversation.

Yet interactivity isn't just a matter of finding and deploying the right technology. Equally if not more important is the need to buttress social media with social *thinking*. Too often, an organization's prevailing culture works against any attempt to transform corporate communication into a two-way affair. For many executives and managers, the temptation to treat every medium at their disposal as if it were a megaphone has proved hard to resist. In some companies, however, leaders have fostered a genuinely interactive culture—values, norms, and behaviors that create a welcoming space for dialogue.

To see how interactivity works, consider Cisco Systems. As it happens, Cisco makes and sells various products that fall under the social technology umbrella. In using them internally, its people have explored the benefits of enabling high-quality back-and-forth communication. One such product, TelePresence, simulates an in-person meeting by beaming video feeds between locations. Multiple large screens create a wraparound effect, and specially designed meeting tables (in an ideal configuration) mirror one another so that users feel as if they were seated at the same piece of furniture. In one sense this is a more robust version of a web-based video chat, with none of the delays or hiccups that typically mar online video. More important, it masters the critical issue of visual scale. When Cisco engineers studied remote interactions, they found that if the on-screen image of a person is less than 80% of his or her true size, those who see the image are less engaged in talking with that person. TelePresence participants appear life-size and can look one another in the eye.

TelePresence is a sophisticated technology tool, but what it enables is the recovery of immediate, spontaneous give-and-take.

Randy Pond, Cisco's executive vice president of operations, processes, and systems, thinks this type of interaction offers the benefit of the "whole" conversation—a concept he illustrated for us with an anecdote. Sitting at his desk for a video conference one day, he could see video feeds of several colleagues on his computer screen when he made a comment to the group and a participant "just put his head in his hands"—presumably in dismay, and presumably not considering that Pond could see him. "I said, 'I can see you,'" Pond told us. "'If you disagree, *tell me.*'" Pond was then able to engage with his skeptical colleague to get the "whole story." A less interactive form of communication might have produced such information eventually—but far less efficiently.

At the crux of Cisco's communication culture is its CEO, John Chambers, who holds various forums to keep in touch with employees. About every other month, for instance, he leads a "birthday chat," open to any Cisco employee whose birthday falls in the relevant two-month period. Senior managers aren't invited, lest their presence keep attendees from speaking openly. Chambers also records a video blog about once a month—a brief, improvisational message delivered by e-mail to all employees. The use of video allows him to speak to his people directly, informally, and without a script; it suggests immediacy and builds trust. And despite the inherently one-way nature of a video blog, Chambers and his team have made it interactive by inviting video messages as well as text comments from employees.

Inclusion: Expanding Employees' Roles

At its best, personal conversation is an equal-opportunity endeavor. It enables participants to share ownership of the substance of their discussion. As a consequence, they can put their own ideas—and, indeed, their hearts and souls—into the conversational arena. Organizational conversation, by the same token, calls on employees to participate in generating the content that makes up a company's story. Inclusive leaders, by counting employees among a company's official or quasi-official communicators, turn those employees into full-fledged conversation partners. In the process, such leaders raise the level of emotional engagement that employees bring to company life in general.

Inclusion adds a critical dimension to the elements of intimacy and interactivity. Whereas intimacy involves the efforts of leaders to get closer to employees, inclusion focuses on the role that employees play in that process. It also extends the practice of interactivity by enabling employees to provide their own ideas—often on official company channels—rather than simply parrying the ideas that others present. It enables them to serve as frontline *content providers.*

In the standard corporate communication model, top executives and professional communicators monopolize the creation of content and keep a tight rein on what people write or say on official company channels. But when a spirit of inclusion takes hold, engaged employees can adopt important new roles, creating content themselves and acting as brand ambassadors, thought leaders, and storytellers.

Brand ambassadors.

When employees feel passionate about their company's products and services, they become living representatives of the brand. This can and does happen organically—lots of people love what they do for a living and will talk it up on their own time. But some companies actively promote that kind of behavior. Coca-Cola, for instance, has created a formal ambassadorship program, aimed at encouraging employees to promote the Coke image and product line in speech and in practice. The Coke intranet provides resources such as a tool that connects employees to company-sponsored volunteer activities. The centerpiece of the program is a list of nine ambassadorial behaviors, which include helping the company "win at the point of sale" (by taking it on themselves to tidy store displays in retail outlets, for example), relaying sales leads, and reporting instances in which a retailer has run out of a Coke product.

Thought leaders.

To achieve market leadership in a knowledge-based field, companies may rely on consultants or in-house professionals to draft speeches, articles, white papers, and the like. But often the most innovative thinking occurs deep within an organization, where people develop and test new products and services. Empowering those people to create and promote thought-leadership material can be a smart, quick way to bolster a company's reputation among key industry players. In recent years Juniper Networks has sponsored initiatives to get potential thought leaders out of their labs and offices and into public venues where industry experts and customers can watch them strut their intellectual stuff. The company's engineers are working on the next wave of systems silicon and hardware and can offer keen insights into trends. To communicate their perspective to relevant audiences, Juniper dispatches them to national and international technology conferences and arranges for them to meet with customers at company-run briefing centers.

Storytellers.
People are accustomed to hearing corporate communication professionals tell stories about a company, but there's nothing like hearing a story direct from the front lines. When employees speak from their own experience, unedited, the message comes to life. The computer storage giant EMC actively elicits stories from its people. Leaders look to them for ideas on how to improve business performance and for thoughts about the company itself. The point is to instill the notion that ideas are welcome from all corners. As just one example, in 2009 the company published *The Working Mother Experience*—a 250-page coffee-table book written by and for EMCers on the topic of being both a successful EMC employee and a parent. The project, initiated at the front lines, was championed by Frank Hauck, then the executive vice president of global marketing and customer quality. It's not unusual for a big company like EMC to produce such a book as a vanity project, but this was no corporate communication effort; it was a peer-driven endeavor, led by employees. Several dozen EMCers also write blogs, many on public sites, expressing their unfiltered thoughts about life at the company and sharing their ideas about technology.

Of course, inclusion means that executives cede a fair amount of control over how the company is represented to the world. But the fact is that cultural and technological changes have eroded that control anyway. Whether you like it or not, anybody can tarnish (or polish) your company's reputation right from her cube, merely by e-mailing an internal document to a reporter, a blogger, or even a group of friends—or by posting her thoughts in an online forum. Thus inclusive leaders are making a virtue out of necessity. Scott Huennekens, the CEO of Volcano Corporation, suggests that a looser approach to communication has made organizational life less stifling and more productive than it used to be. The free flow of information creates a freer spirit. Some companies do try to set some basic expectations. Infosys, for instance, acknowledging its lack of control over employees' participation in social networks, tells employees that they may disagree but asks them not to be *disagreeable*.

And quite often, leaders have discovered, a system of self-regulation by employees fills the void left by top-down control. Somebody comes out with an outrageous statement, the community responds, and the overall sentiment swings back to the middle.

Intentionality: Pursuing an Agenda

A personal conversation, if it's truly rich and rewarding, will be open but not aimless; the participants will have some sense of what they hope to achieve. They might seek to entertain each other, or to persuade each other, or to learn from each other. In the absence of such intent, a conversation will either meander or run into a blind alley. Intent confers order and meaning on even the loosest and most digressive forms of chatter. That principle applies to organizational conversation, too. Over time, the many voices that contribute to the process of communication within a company must converge on a single vision of what that communication is *for*. To put it another way: The conversation that unfolds within a company should reflect a shared agenda that aligns with the company's strategic objectives.

Intentionality differs from the other three elements of organizational conversation in one key respect. While intimacy, interactivity, and inclusion all serve to open up the flow of information and ideas within a company, intentionality brings a measure of closure to that process: It enables leaders and employees to derive strategically relevant action from the push and pull of discussion and debate.

Conversational intentionality requires leaders to convey strategic principles not just by asserting them but by explaining them—by generating consent rather than commanding assent. In this new model, leaders speak extensively and explicitly with employees about the vision and the logic that underlie executive decision making. As a result, people at every level gain a big-picture view of where their company stands within its competitive environment. In short, they become *conversant* in matters of organizational strategy.

One way to help employees understand the company's governing strategy is to let them have a part in creating it. The leadership team at Infosys has taken to including a broad range of employees in the company's annual strategy-development process. In late 2009, as Infosys leaders began to build an organizational strategy for the 2011 fiscal year, they invited people from every rank and division of the company to join in. In particular, explains Kris Gopalakrishnan, a cofounder and executive cochairman, they asked employees to submit ideas on "the significant transformational trends that we see affecting our customers." Using those ideas, strategic planners at Infosys came up with a list of 17 trends, ranging from the growth of emerging markets to the increasing emphasis on environmental sustainability. They then created a series of online forums in which employees could suggest how to match each trend with various customer solutions that the company might offer. Technology and social networks enabled bottom-up participation across the company.

In 2008 Kingfisher plc, the world's third-largest home improvement retailer, began pursuing a new strategy to transform a group of historically discrete business units into "one team," in part through intentional organizational conversation. To launch the effort, company leaders held a three-day event in Barcelona for retail executives. On the second day everyone participated in a 90-minute session called Share at the Marketplace, which was intended to emulate a classic Mediterranean or Middle Eastern bazaar. One group of participants, called "suppliers," donned aprons, and each person stood at one of 22 stalls, ready to give a spiel about a business practice developed by people in his or her part of the Kingfisher organization. Essentially they were purveyors of ideas.

Another group—executive committee members—served as facilitators, ambling through the aisles and providing words of encouragement. The third and largest group acted as buyers, moving from one stall to the next, examining the "merchandise," and occasionally "purchasing" one of the ideas. Using special checkbooks issued for this purpose, buyers could draft up to five checks each to pay for suppliers' wares. Such transactions had no force beyond the confines of the session, but they conveyed a strong message to the suppliers: What you're telling me is impressive. The essence of the marketplace was the peer-to-peer sharing of best practices in an informal, messy, and noisy environment. But the idea was also to treat conversation as a means to an end—to use it to achieve strategic alignment across a diverse group of participants.

Conversation goes on in every company, whether you recognize it or not. That has always been the case, but today the conversation has the potential to spread well beyond your walls, and it's largely out of your control. Smart leaders find ways to use conversation—to manage the flow of information in an honest, open fashion. One-way broadcast messaging is a relic, and slick marketing materials have as little effect on employees as they do on customers. But people will listen to communication that is intimate, interactive, inclusive, and intentional.

Originally published in June 2012. Reprint R1206D

The Surprising Power of Questions

by Alison Wood Brooks and Leslie K. John

MUCH OF AN EXECUTIVE'S WORKDAY is spent asking others for information—requesting status updates from a team leader, for example, or questioning a counterpart in a tense negotiation. Yet unlike professionals such as litigators, journalists, and doctors, who are taught how to ask questions as an essential part of their training, few executives think of questioning as a skill that can be honed—or consider how their own answers to questions could make conversations more productive.

That's a missed opportunity. Questioning is a uniquely powerful tool for unlocking value in organizations: It spurs learning and the exchange of ideas, it fuels innovation and performance improvement, it builds rapport and trust among team members. And it can mitigate business risk by uncovering unforeseen pitfalls and hazards.

For some people, questioning comes easily. Their natural inquisitiveness, emotional intelligence, and ability to read people put the ideal question on the tip of their tongue. But most of us don't ask enough questions, nor do we pose our inquiries in an optimal way.

The good news is that by asking questions, we naturally improve our emotional intelligence, which in turn makes us better questioners—a virtuous cycle. In this article, we draw on insights from behavioral science research to explore how the way we frame questions and choose to answer our counterparts can influence the outcome of conversations. We offer guidance for choosing the best type, tone, sequence, and framing of questions and for deciding what and how much information to share to reap the most benefit from our interactions, not just for ourselves but for our organizations.

Don't Ask, Don't Get

"Be a good listener," Dale Carnegie advised in his 1936 classic *How to Win Friends and Influence People.* "Ask questions the other person will enjoy answering." More than 80 years later, most people still fail to heed Carnegie's sage advice. When one of us (Alison) began studying conversations at Harvard Business School several years ago, she quickly arrived at a foundational insight: People don't ask enough questions. In fact, among the most common complaints people make after having a conversation, such as an interview, a first date, or a work meeting, is "I wish [s/he] had asked me more questions" and "I can't believe [s/he] didn't ask me any questions."

Why do so many of us hold back? There are many reasons. People may be egocentric—eager to impress others with their own thoughts, stories, and ideas (and not even think to ask questions). Perhaps they are apathetic—they don't care enough to ask, or they anticipate being bored by the answers they'd hear. They may be overconfident in their own knowledge and think they already know the answers (which sometimes they do, but usually not). Or perhaps they worry that they'll ask the wrong question and be viewed as rude or incompetent. But the biggest inhibitor, in our opinion, is that most people just don't understand how beneficial good questioning can be. If they did, they would end far fewer sentences with a period—and more with a question mark.

Dating back to the 1970s, research suggests that people have conversations to accomplish some combination of two major goals: information exchange (learning) and impression management (liking). Recent research shows that asking questions achieves both. Alison and Harvard colleagues Karen Huang, Michael Yeomans, Julia Minson, and Francesca Gino scrutinized thousands of natural conversations among participants who were getting to know each other, either in online chats or on in-person speed dates. The

Idea in Brief

The Problem

Some professionals such as litigators, journalists, and even doctors are taught to ask questions as part of their training. But few executives think about questioning as a skill that can be honed. That's a missed opportunity.

The Opportunity

Questioning is a powerful tool for unlocking value in companies: It spurs learning and the exchange of ideas, it fuels innovation and better performance, it builds trust among team members. And it can mitigate business risk by uncovering unforeseen pitfalls and hazards.

The Approach

Several techniques can enhance the power and efficacy of queries: Favor follow-up questions, know when to keep questions open-ended, get the sequence right, use the right tone, and pay attention to group dynamics.

researchers told some people to ask many questions (at least nine in fifteen minutes) and others to ask very few (no more than four in fifteen minutes). In the online chats, the people who were randomly assigned to ask many questions were better liked by their conversation partners and learned more about their partners' interests. For example, when quizzed about their partners' preferences for activities such as reading, cooking, and exercising, high question askers were more likely to be able to guess correctly. Among the speed daters, people were more willing to go on a second date with partners who asked more questions. In fact, asking just one more question on each date meant that participants persuaded one additional person (over the course of 20 dates) to go out with them again.

Questions are such powerful tools that they can be beneficial—perhaps particularly so—in circumstances when question asking goes against social norms. For instance, prevailing norms tell us that job candidates are expected to answer questions during interviews. But research by Dan Cable, at the London Business School, and Virginia Kay, at the University of North Carolina, suggests that most people excessively self-promote during job interviews. And when interviewees focus on selling themselves, they are likely to forget to ask questions—about the interviewer, the organization, the work—that would make the interviewer feel more engaged and more apt to view the candidate favorably and could help the candidate predict whether the job would provide satisfying work. For job candidates, asking questions such as "What am I not asking you that I should?" can signal competence, build rapport, and unlock key pieces of information about the position.

Most people don't grasp that asking a lot of questions unlocks learning and improves interpersonal bonding. In Alison's studies, for example, though people could accurately recall how many questions had been asked in their conversations, they didn't intuit the link between questions and liking. Across four studies, in which participants were engaged in conversations themselves or read transcripts of others' conversations, people tended not to realize that question asking would influence—or had influenced—the level of amity between the conversationalists.

The New Socratic Method

The first step in becoming a better questioner is simply to ask more questions. Of course, the sheer number of questions is not the only factor that influences the quality of a conversation: The type, tone, sequence, and framing also matter.

In our teaching at Harvard Business School, we run an exercise in which we instruct pairs of students to have a conversation. Some students are told to ask as few questions as possible, and some are instructed to ask as many as possible. Among the low-low pairs (both students ask a minimum of questions), participants generally report that the experience is a bit like children engaging in parallel play: They exchange statements but struggle to initiate an interactive, enjoyable, or productive dialogue. The high-high pairs find that too many questions can also create a stilted dynamic. However, the high-low pairs' experiences are mixed. Sometimes the question asker learns a lot about her partner, the answerer feels heard, and both come away feeling profoundly closer. Other times, one of the participants may feel uncomfortable in his role or unsure about how much to share, and the conversation can feel like an interrogation.

Our research suggests several approaches that can enhance the power and efficacy of queries. The best approach for a given situation depends on the goals of the conversationalists—specifically, whether the discussion is cooperative (for example, the duo is trying to build a relationship or accomplish a task together) or competitive (the parties seek to uncover sensitive information from each other or serve their own interests), or some combination of both. (See the exhibit "Conversational Goals Matter.") Consider the following tactics.

Favor follow-up questions.

Not all questions are created equal. Alison's research, using human coding and machine learning, revealed four types of questions: introductory questions ("How are you?"), mirror questions ("I'm fine. How are you?"), full-switch questions (ones that change the topic entirely), and follow-up questions (ones that solicit more information). Although each type is abundant in natural conversation, follow-up questions seem to have special power. They signal to your conversation partner that you are listening, care, and want to know more. People interacting with a partner who asks lots of follow-up questions tend to feel respected and heard.

An unexpected benefit of follow-up questions is that they don't require much thought or preparation—indeed, they seem to come naturally to interlocutors. In Alison's studies, the people who were told to ask more questions used more follow-up questions than any other type without being instructed to do so.

Know when to keep questions open-ended.

No one likes to feel interrogated—and some types of questions can force answerers into a yes-or-no corner. Open-ended questions can counteract that effect and thus can be particularly useful in uncovering information or learning something new. Indeed, they are wellsprings of innovation—which is often the result of finding the hidden, unexpected answer that no one has thought of before.

A wealth of research in survey design has shown the dangers of narrowing respondents' options. For example, "closed" questions

Conversational goals matter

Conversations fall along a continuum from purely competitive to purely co-operative. For example, discussions about the allocation of scarce resources tend to be competitive; those between friends and colleagues are generally cooperative; and others, such as managers' check-ins with employees, are mixed—supportive but also providing feedback and communicating expectations. Here are some challenges that commonly arise when asking and answering questions and tactics for handling them.

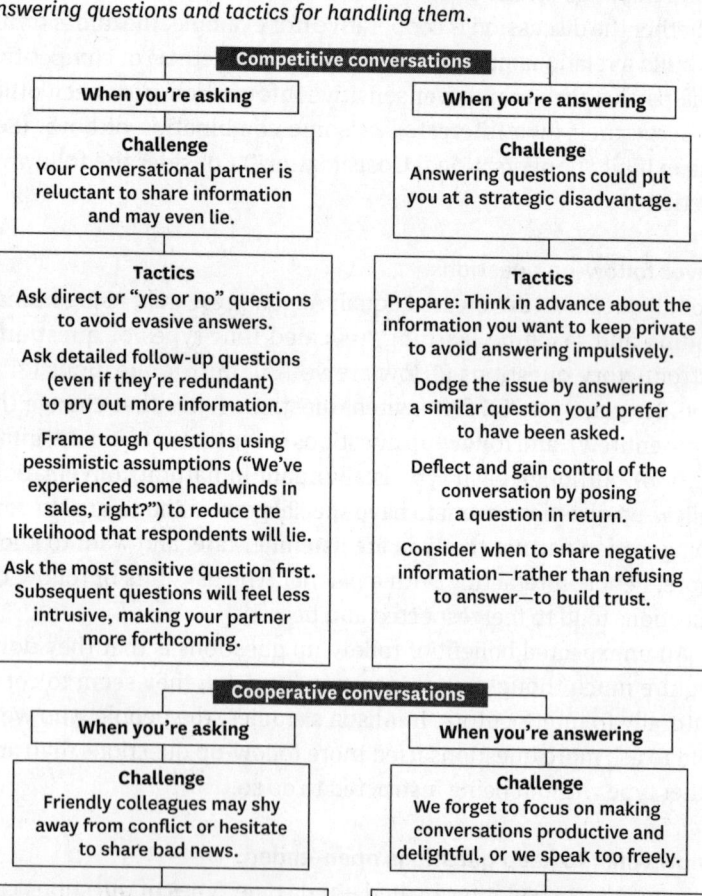

Competitive conversations

When you're asking

Challenge
Your conversational partner is reluctant to share information and may even lie.

Tactics
Ask direct or "yes or no" questions to avoid evasive answers.

Ask detailed follow-up questions (even if they're redundant) to pry out more information.

Frame tough questions using pessimistic assumptions ("We've experienced some headwinds in sales, right?") to reduce the likelihood that respondents will lie.

Ask the most sensitive question first. Subsequent questions will feel less intrusive, making your partner more forthcoming.

When you're answering

Challenge
Answering questions could put you at a strategic disadvantage.

Tactics
Prepare: Think in advance about the information you want to keep private to avoid answering impulsively.

Dodge the issue by answering a similar question you'd prefer to have been asked.

Deflect and gain control of the conversation by posing a question in return.

Consider when to share negative information—rather than refusing to answer—to build trust.

Cooperative conversations

When you're asking

Challenge
Friendly colleagues may shy away from conflict or hesitate to share bad news.

Tactics
Ask open-ended questions ("If you were to play devil's advocate, what would you say?") to draw out negative feedback.

Begin with the least-sensitive questions to build rapport, and escalate slowly.

As in competitive contexts, frame tough questions using negative assumptions.

When you're answering

Challenge
We forget to focus on making conversations productive and delightful, or we speak too freely.

Tactics
Avoid droning on and on. Use energy, humor, and storytelling to engage your partners.

Avoid talking too much about yourself, and remember to ask questions of others.

Deflect tough questions by answering with another question or a joke.

can introduce bias and manipulation. In one study, in which parents were asked what they deemed "the most important thing for children to prepare them in life," about 60% of them chose "to think for themselves" from a list of response options. However, when the same question was asked in an open-ended format, only about 5% of parents spontaneously came up with an answer along those lines.

Of course, open-ended questions aren't always optimal. For example, if you are in a tense negotiation or are dealing with people who tend to keep their cards close to their chest, open-ended questions can leave too much wiggle room, inviting them to dodge or lie by omission. In such situations, closed questions work better, especially if they are framed correctly. For example, research by Julia Minson, the University of Utah's Eric VanEpps, Georgetown's Jeremy Yip, and Wharton's Maurice Schweitzer indicates that people are less likely to lie if questioners make pessimistic assumptions ("This business will need some new equipment soon, correct?") rather than optimistic ones ("The equipment is in good working order, right?").

Sometimes the information you wish to ascertain is so sensitive that direct questions won't work, no matter how thoughtfully they are framed. In these situations, a survey tactic can aid discovery. In research Leslie conducted with Alessandro Acquisti and George Loewenstein of Carnegie Mellon University, she found that people were more forthcoming when requests for sensitive information were couched within another task—in the study's case, rating the ethicality of antisocial behaviors such as cheating on one's tax return or letting a drunk friend drive home. Participants were asked to rate the ethicality using one scale if they had engaged in a particular behavior and another scale if they hadn't—thus revealing which antisocial acts they themselves had engaged in. Although this tactic may sometimes prove useful at an organizational level—we can imagine that managers might administer a survey rather than ask workers directly about sensitive information such as salary expectations—we counsel restraint in using it. If people feel that you are trying to trick them into revealing something, they may lose trust in you, decreasing the likelihood that they'll share information in the future and potentially eroding workplace relationships.

Get the sequence right.

The optimal order of your questions depends on the circumstances. During tense encounters, asking tough questions first, even if it feels socially awkward to do so, can make your conversational partner more willing to open up. Leslie and her coauthors found that people are more willing to reveal sensitive information when questions are asked in a decreasing order of intrusiveness. When a question asker begins with a highly sensitive question—such as "Have you ever had a fantasy of doing something terrible to someone?"—subsequent questions, such as "Have you ever called in sick to work when you were perfectly healthy?" feel, by comparison, less intrusive, and thus we tend to be more forthcoming. Of course, if the first question is *too* sensitive, you run the risk of offending your counterpart. So it's a delicate balance, to be sure.

If the goal is to build relationships, the opposite approach—opening with less sensitive questions and escalating slowly—seems to be most effective. In a classic set of studies (the results of which went viral following a write-up in the "Modern Love" column of the *New York Times*), psychologist Arthur Aron recruited strangers to come to the lab, paired them up, and gave them a list of questions. They were told to work their way through the list, starting with relatively shallow inquiries and progressing to more self-revelatory ones, such as "What is your biggest regret?" Pairs in the control group were asked simply to interact with each other. The pairs who followed the prescribed structure liked each other more than the control pairs. This effect is so strong that it has been formalized in a task called "the relationship closeness induction," a tool used by researchers to build a sense of connection among experiment participants.

Good interlocutors also understand that questions asked previously in a conversation can influence future queries. For example, Norbert Schwarz, of the University of Southern California, and his coauthors found that when the question "How satisfied are you with your life?" is followed by the question "How satisfied are you with your marriage?" the answers were highly correlated: Respondents who reported being satisfied with their life also said they were

The Power of Questions in Sales

THERE ARE FEW BUSINESS SETTINGS in which asking questions is more important than sales. A recent study of more than 500,000 business-to-business sales conversations—over the phone and via online platforms—by tech company Gong.io reveals that top-performing salespeople ask questions differently than their peers.

Consistent with past research, the data shows a strong connection between the number of questions a salesperson asks and his or her sales conversion rate (in terms of both securing the next meeting and eventually closing the deal). This is true even after controlling for the gender of the salesperson and the call type (demo, proposal, negotiation, and so on). However, there is a point of diminishing returns. Conversion rates start to drop off after about 14 questions, with 11 to 14 being the optimal range.

The data also shows that top-performing salespeople tend to scatter questions throughout the sales call, which makes it feel more like a conversation than an interrogation. Lower performers, in contrast, frontload questions in the first half of the sales call, as if they're making their way through a to-do list.

Just as important, top salespeople listen more and speak less than their counterparts overall. Taken together, the data from Gong.io affirms what great salespeople intuitively understand: When sellers ask questions rather than just make their pitch, they close more deals.

---

satisfied with their marriage. When asked the questions in this order, people implicitly interpreted that life satisfaction "ought to be" closely tied to marriage. However, when the same questions were asked in the opposite order, the answers were less closely correlated.

Use the right tone.
People are more forthcoming when you ask questions in a casual way, rather than in a buttoned-up, official tone. In one of Leslie's studies, participants were posed a series of sensitive questions in an online survey. For one group of participants, the website's user interface looked fun and frivolous; for another group, the site looked official. (The control group was presented with a neutral-looking site.) Participants were about twice as likely to reveal sensitive information on the casual-looking site than on the others.

People also tend to be more forthcoming when given an escape hatch or "out" in a conversation. For example, if they are told that they can change their answers at any point, they tend to open up more—even though they rarely end up making changes. This might explain why teams and groups find brainstorming sessions so productive. In a whiteboard setting, where anything can be erased and judgment is suspended, people are more likely to answer questions honestly and say things they otherwise might not. Of course, there will be times when an off-the-cuff approach is inappropriate. But in general, an overly formal tone is likely to inhibit people's willingness to share information.

Pay attention to group dynamics.
Conversational dynamics can change profoundly depending on whether you're chatting one-on-one with someone or talking in a group. Not only is the willingness to answer questions affected simply by the presence of others, but members of a group tend to follow one another's lead. In one set of studies, Leslie and her coauthors asked participants a series of sensitive questions, including ones about finances ("Have you ever bounced a check?") and sex ("While an adult, have you ever felt sexual desire for a minor?"). Participants were told either that most others in the study were willing to reveal stigmatizing answers or that they were unwilling to do so. Participants who were told that others had been forthcoming were 27% likelier to reveal sensitive answers than those who were told that others had been reticent. In a meeting or group setting, it takes only a few closed-off people for questions to lose their probing power. The opposite is true, too. As soon as one person starts to open up, the rest of the group is likely to follow suit.

Group dynamics can also affect how a question asker is perceived. Alison's research reveals that participants in a conversation enjoy being asked questions and tend to like the people asking questions more than those who answer them. But when third-party observers watch the same conversation unfold, they prefer the person who answers questions. This makes sense: People who mostly ask questions tend to disclose very little about themselves or their thoughts.

To those listening to a conversation, question askers may come across as defensive, evasive, or invisible, while those answering seem more fascinating, present, or memorable.

The Best Response

A conversation is a dance that requires partners to be in sync—it's a mutual push-and-pull that unfolds over time. Just as the way we ask questions can facilitate trust and the sharing of information—so, too, can the way we answer them.

Answering questions requires making a choice about where to fall on a continuum between privacy and transparency. Should we answer the question? If we answer, how forthcoming should we be? What should we do when asked a question that, if answered truthfully, might reveal a less-than-glamorous fact or put us in a disadvantaged strategic position? Each end of the spectrum—fully opaque and fully transparent—has benefits and pitfalls. Keeping information private can make us feel free to experiment and learn. In negotiations, withholding sensitive information (such as the fact that your alternatives are weak) can help you secure better outcomes. At the same time, transparency is an essential part of forging meaningful connections. Even in a negotiation context, transparency can lead to value-creating deals; by sharing information, participants can identify elements that are relatively unimportant to one party but important to the other—the foundation of a win-win outcome.

And keeping secrets has costs. Research by Julie Lane and Daniel Wegner, of the University of Virginia, suggests that concealing secrets during social interactions leads to the intrusive recurrence of secret thoughts, while research by Columbia's Michael Slepian, Jinseok Chun, and Malia Mason shows that keeping secrets—even outside of social interactions—depletes us cognitively, interferes with our ability to concentrate and remember things, and even harms long-term health and well-being.

In an organizational context, people too often err on the side of privacy—and underappreciate the benefits of transparency. How often do we realize that we could have truly bonded with a colleague only after he or she has moved on to a new company? Why are better deals often uncovered after the ink has dried, the tension has broken, and negotiators begin to chat freely?

To maximize the benefits of answering questions—and minimize the risks—it's important to decide before a conversation begins what information you want to share and what you want to keep private.

Deciding what to share.

There is no rule of thumb for how much—or what type—of information you should disclose. Indeed, transparency is such a powerful bonding agent that sometimes it doesn't matter what is revealed—even information that reflects poorly on us can draw our conversational partners closer. In research Leslie conducted with HBS collaborators Kate Barasz and Michael Norton, she found that most people assume that it would be less damaging to refuse to answer a question that would reveal negative information—for example, "Have you ever been reprimanded at work?"—than to answer affirmatively. But this intuition is wrong. When they asked people to take the perspective of a recruiter and choose between two candidates (equivalent except for how they responded to this question), nearly 90% preferred the candidate who "came clean" and answered the question. Before a conversation takes place, think carefully about whether refusing to answer tough questions would do more harm than good.

Deciding what to keep private.

Of course, at times you and your organization would be better served by keeping your cards close to your chest. In our negotiation classes, we teach strategies for handling hard questions without lying. Dodging, or answering a question you *wish* you had been asked, can be effective not only in helping you protect information you'd rather keep private but also in building a good rapport with your conversational partner, especially if you speak eloquently. In a study led by Todd Rogers, of Harvard's Kennedy School, participants were shown clips of political candidates responding to questions by either answering them or dodging them. Eloquent dodgers were liked more than ineloquent answerers, but only when their dodges went undetected. Another effective strategy is deflecting, or answering a probing question with another question or a joke. Answerers can use this approach to lead the conversation in a different direction.

———————————

"Question everything," Albert Einstein famously said. Personal creativity and organizational innovation rely on a willingness to seek out novel information. Questions and thoughtful answers foster smoother and more-effective interactions; they strengthen rapport and trust and lead groups toward discovery. All this we have documented in our research. But we believe questions and answers have a power that goes far beyond matters of performance. The wellspring of all questions is wonder and curiosity and a capacity for delight. We pose and respond to queries in the belief that the magic of a conversation will produce a whole that is greater than the sum of its parts. Sustained personal engagement and motivation—in our lives as well as our work—require that we are always mindful of the transformative joy of asking and answering questions.

Originally published in May–June 2018. Reprint R1803C

A Second Chance to Make the Right Impression

by Heidi Grant

YEARS AGO A FRIEND OF MINE, GORDON, interviewed for a position at a prominent university. During his daylong visit to campus, he had lunch with a senior faculty member (let's call him Bob) who had final say over the hire. After their food arrived, Bob said of his meal, "You know, this is great. You should try this." Even though Gordon knew it was a dish he wouldn't like, he felt pressured to have a bite so as not to offend his potential future boss. The lunch continued pleasantly, with Gordon enumerating his accomplishments and Bob responding positively. Gordon was therefore more than a little surprised when he didn't get the job.

He learned why a few years later, after he'd been hired for a different position at the same university. Apparently, when Bob had said "You should try this," he had actually meant something like "You should try this *sometime*" or "My lunch is excellent," and he was deeply disturbed that a job candidate would have the audacity to eat right from his plate. He had no desire to work with someone so disrespectful and ill-mannered.

Gordon's experience is an example of an all-too-common problem: unwittingly making a bad first impression.

Not coming across as you intend—particularly in your initial encounter with someone—can cause big problems in your personal and professional life. People may mistrust you, dislike you, or not even notice you. Sometimes the fault is your own: You screwed up and you know it. But more often than not, bad first impressions stem from certain biases in how people perceive one another. And this happens routinely: Research shows only weak correlations between what others think of us and how we see ourselves. So if you've ever felt underestimated, sensed that you inadvertently stepped on toes, or thought that false and hurtful assumptions were being made about you, you were probably right. The way we see one another can be irrational, incomplete, and inflexible—and largely (but not entirely) automatic.

To be fair, perceiving people accurately is hard. No one is truly an "open book." Studies show that although strong basic emotions—surprise, fear, disgust, and anger—are fairly easy to read, the more subtle emotions we experience daily are not. So how you look when you're slightly frustrated probably isn't all that different from how you look when you are a little concerned, confused, disappointed, or nervous. Your "I'm kind of hurt by what you just said" face probably looks a lot like your "I'm not at all hurt by what you just said" face. And the majority of times that you've thought, "I made my intentions clear" or "They know what I meant," you didn't and they don't. Psychologists call this disconnect the *transparency illusion*.

It's important to understand that your words and behaviors are always subject to interpretation. Imagine that you're at a meeting, and you begin staring off into space while a colleague is speaking. Are you bored? Are you thinking deeply about what she is saying? Are you wondering if you remembered to turn off the coffeepot? Your colleague has no way of knowing why you are behaving as you are, but she will pick an interpretation—because that's what our brains do.

There is good news, however. We now know that errors in reading people are highly predictable, because perception is governed by rules and biases we can identify and anticipate. It is therefore possible to ensure that you're making the right impression more often, and to correct any misperceptions that others have about you.

Idea in Brief

All too often, when we think we're projecting a certain image to others, they perceive us very differently. This happens in part because people tend to make judgments unconsciously and automatically, influenced by various biases. But research from social psychologists can help us understand the flaws in human perception and make sure we're judged fairly.

According to the author, someone meeting you for the first time—or reassessing you later—is likely to be viewing you through various lenses:

- the trust lens, to decide if you are friend or foe;

- the power lens, to assess your usefulness; and

- the ego lens, to confirm a sense of superiority.

Grant suggests specific ways you can use this information to put your best foot forward or overcome a bad impression, including projecting warmth and competence, demonstrating your instrumentality in reaching someone's goals, and being modest and inclusive.

By thinking strategically about how we all form our impressions, you'll find it much easier to come across as you intend and be seen in a favorable light.

Understanding Perception

Any new person you encounter—a potential boss, a prospective client, a new colleague—is likely to evaluate you in two phases. In phase one, the person makes an initial assessment of you quickly and without conscious thought, relying on a variety of heuristics, stereotypes, and other assumptions—using cues like your physical appearance, your organizational role, and your body language to fill in the blanks. This is less out of laziness (though there is some of that) than out of necessity. In a brief first meeting, the perceiver has too much to notice, understand, and act on to give you undivided, unbiased attention. In phase two—if there *is* a phase two—the perceiver has to work a lot harder, paying closer attention, gathering disparate data, and making sense of it to draw informed, thoughtful conclusions about you. It takes serious mental effort to weigh all the possible factors influencing your behavior and to reconsider the snap judgments made in phase one. So the perceiver needs to be motivated to do it and not too distracted.

In both phases, but particularly the first, the people forming an impression of you aren't simply passive observers. They have, without necessarily realizing it, particular questions they are trying to answer about you. It's as if they are looking through a distinct lens, or set of lenses, that shapes their view of you. The most powerful of these are the trust, power, and ego lenses. (Additional lenses, driven by personality, might also be present, but they're typically less important; see the sidebar "Other Lenses of Perception.")

The *trust lens* is employed when people want to figure out if you are friend or foe. Perceivers answer that question by tuning in to two particular aspects of your character: your warmth (your expression of friendliness, respect, and empathy), which suggests that you have good intentions, and your competence (evidence that you are intelligent, skilled, and effective), which shows that you can act on your intentions.

The *power lens* comes into play when there is a disparity of power, especially when the perceiver has more than you do. He or she gazes through this lens to assess your instrumentality: "Prove yourself useful to me, or get out of my way."

The *ego lens* gives the perceiver a sense of who's on top. Subconsciously, people often want confirmation that they, or their group, are superior to other individuals or groups.

Turning back to Gordon, there are several ways in which Bob's lenses no doubt influenced the outcome of the lunch interview. Gordon readily displayed his competence by reviewing his track record, but he failed to show warmth—indeed, the misunderstanding that led him to sample Bob's food ended up conveying a lack of respect. Competence without warmth is a terrible combination, because it suggests that you may one day be a potent foe. Also, in focusing solely on his own accomplishments while talking with someone more powerful, Gordon failed to emphasize his instrumentality. If he had better explained how his previous experience would help him to further Bob's goals at the university, it might have been a whole different ball game. As it was, looking through his trust, power, and ego lenses, Bob probably thought, Why hire an accomplished outsider who might work against me and make me look bad?

Coming Across the Right Way

So how can you use this knowledge of perception and its lenses to your advantage and consistently and effectively telegraph your intended messages? The first and most obvious strategy is to present the right kinds of evidence to help others draw the correct impression, keeping the lenses of perception in mind.

To get someone to see you accurately through her trust lens, project warmth and competence. Give the right physical signals: Make eye contact, smile when appropriate, nod in agreement, listen carefully without interrupting, sit up straight, and stand tall. And, especially if this is to be a lasting relationship, be a person of your word. Those who are perceived as principled and reliable are the most likely to be seen as strong allies.

To create the right impression in your perceiver's power lens, be sure to demonstrate your instrumentality at every reasonable opportunity. Make it clear that you want to help her be more effective in reaching your mutual goals.

And to be seen positively through her ego lens, be modest and inclusive. Go out of your way to affirm the strengths of others, and try to create a sense of "us," so that your perceiver can celebrate your achievements rather than feel threatened by them.

If you started off on the wrong foot and need to overcome a bad impression, the evidence will have to be plentiful and attention-getting in order to activate phase two thinking. Keep piling it on until your perceiver can no longer tune it out, and make sure that the information you're presenting is clearly inconsistent with the existing ideas about you. For instance, imagine that you missed a deadline on your first assignment for a new manager. Meeting your next deadline might or might not correct his impression of you. But what if you beat the next five deadlines by a week each time? That would certainly register. Your boss would naturally pay closer attention to see if the change lasts, and you would have successfully nudged him into phase two.

Another, complementary approach is to make your perceivers *want* to revise their opinions of you, thereby improving your image faster and with less effort. Here are a few strategies you might try:

Activate the desire to be fair.

Most people will tell you they strive to be open-minded and even-handed in the way they judge and treat others. Psychologists call this having an *egalitarian goal*. Research suggests that when perceivers are genuinely committed to being fair, and when fairness has been recently reinforced in their minds, they will to a large degree spontaneously and automatically inhibit biases that might inappropriately influence their perceptions. It's almost like skipping phase one and heading directly to phase two, where the impression you create will be more accurate and more in keeping with your intentions.

To activate the egalitarian goal, you can compliment your perceiver on his "fairness," "unbiased assessment," "keen perception," or "uncanny accuracy" in evaluating people. If you don't know the person well and would have no basis for making such a judgment, you might suggest that in his line of work or position in the company, the ability to accurately assess others must be a key skill. You wouldn't be lying; most people do need to accurately read colleagues and clients to succeed in their jobs. You can also try sharing your own challenges with fairness. Describe a time when you misjudged someone by letting some kind of bias get in the way. (To my embarrassment, I have a whole catalog of such stories, like the time I nearly called security on a disheveled man in a dirty T-shirt and sweatpants wandering the halls at Columbia. When I saw him again the next month, he was delivering a talk to the entire department on the complex new statistic he had just invented. A noted psychologist and statistician, he would later become one of my mentors.)

Make yourself necessary.

In many ways the easiest and most direct way to get other people to want to perceive you correctly—to make phase two processing worth

Other Lenses of Perception

ALTHOUGH THE TRUST, POWER, and ego lenses are the ones that people use most often to form judgments about others, two sets of lenses specific to personality type can also come into play.

Promotion/Prevention

Does your perceiver tend to embrace risk or steer clear of it? Those with a promotion lens want to maximize gains and avoid missed opportunities, while those with a prevention lens try to minimize losses and maintain the status quo.

Advice: Identify the lens of your perceiver and speak the appropriate motivational language.

Anxious/Avoidant

Does your perceiver have attachment issues? About half of U.S. adults have trouble relating to others. Some people display anxious behavior: They are needy, too accommodating, and sensitive to rejection. Others practice avoidance: They are aloof and struggle to connect.

Advice: If an anxious or avoidant lens is present, be empathetic, patient, and reliable.

their while—is to ensure that you have a role in their success. Psychologists call this *outcome dependency.* In a nutshell, it means that others can't get what they want without cooperation from you. This is why the powerless pay such close attention to the powerful. And this is why individuals who must rely on someone else to deliver will take the trouble to better understand that person's character, intentions, and habits. If your perceiver needs to be able to predict your behavior, anticipate your wants and needs, and respond accordingly, she's got no choice but to enter phase two.

To create outcome dependency, try to identify opportunities for collaboration. For example, if your supervisor has underestimated you, consider asking for an assignment that would allow you to work with her more closely. It's natural to shy away from people who don't think highly of you, but you need to fight that instinct and instead stick to them like glue if you hope to correct their misperceptions.

Things will get much more comfortable once they begin to realize that you're not so bad after all.

Seize the right moments.

Human beings have a deep and fundamental desire for control. Not having it—because of stressors such as uncertainty, lack of choices, coercion, or micromanagement—reliably leads to feelings of helplessness, apathy, and depression. When people experience a loss of control, they naturally try to get it back. And if they can't do that by attacking the problem directly (for example, telling the micromanaging boss "I quit"), research shows that they may become more vigilant and detail-oriented about other matters, including the process of observing others.

You can take advantage of occasions when your perceiver is feeling at the mercy of outside forces: when your boss is stressed about meeting year-end goals, or when a colleague is struggling to complete a project on time or has lost an important client. Focusing on getting to know you better is a way for people to feel as if they're reclaiming control. So just by being present and, if possible, stepping up to help, you can highlight your strengths when your perceiver is most likely to notice.

Are you wondering if Gordon was ever able to overcome that bad first impression he made with Bob? Yes, he was, with an approach that involved several of these strategies. First, he thought long and hard about the work that Bob (now a department head) was doing, and he took every opportunity to reach out and support Bob's agenda. He also made sure to project warmth during their interactions and to express himself with greater humility. After about a year, Bob invited him to participate on several key committees, and Gordon felt that the pair had established a level of trust. Nowadays, they even have friendly lunches once in a while—without sampling each other's food.

We all want to make good impressions that accord with the images we intend to project. Research consistently shows that people are happier and more satisfied and have better relationships and greater feelings of purpose when they believe they come across authentically. Life is simply easier and more rewarding when others "get" you and provide you with the opportunities and support that are a good fit.

But you can't sit back and wait for those around you to accurately size you up. You need to think strategically about encouraging and incentivizing them to see you in the best possible light. If you do, then it is really never too late to make the right impression.

Originally published in January–February 2015. Reprint R1501J

The Art of Giving and Receiving Advice

by David A. Garvin and Joshua D. Margolis

SEEKING AND GIVING advice are central to effective leadership and decision making. Yet managers seldom view them as practical skills they can learn and improve. Receiving guidance is often seen as the passive consumption of wisdom. And advising is typically treated as a matter of "good judgment"—you either have it or you don't—rather than a competency to be mastered.

When the exchange is done well, people on both sides of the table benefit. Those who are truly open to guidance (and not just looking for validation) develop better solutions to problems than they would have on their own. They add nuance and texture to their thinking—and, research shows, they can overcome cognitive biases, self-serving rationales, and other flaws in their logic. Those who give advice effectively wield soft influence—they shape important decisions while empowering others to act. As engaged listeners, they can also learn a lot from the problems that people bring them. And the rule of reciprocity is a powerful binding force: Providing expert advice often creates an implicit debt that recipients will want to repay.

But advice seekers and givers must clear significant hurdles, such as a deeply ingrained tendency to prefer their own opinions, irrespective of their merit, and the fact that careful listening is hard, time-consuming work. The whole interaction is a subtle and intricate art. On both sides it requires emotional intelligence, self-awareness, restraint, diplomacy, and patience. The process can derail in many ways, and getting it wrong can have damaging consequences—misunderstanding and frustration, decision gridlock, subpar solutions, frayed relationships, and thwarted personal development—with substantial costs to individuals and their organizations.

Because these essential skills are assumed to emerge organically, they're rarely taught; but we've found that they can be learned and applied to great effect. So we've drawn on extensive research (ours and others') to identify the most common obstacles and some practical guidelines for getting past them. Though heavily disguised, the examples in this article are based on interviewees' real experiences in a range of settings. Of course, advice takes different forms in different circumstances. (See the table "Know what's called for.") Coaching and mentoring are covered extensively elsewhere, so here we focus on situations that involve big, risky, or emotionally charged decisions—those in which you might consult with someone multiple times—because leaders struggle with such decisions and must learn to handle them well.

Why This Is Harder Than It Looks

Whether you're receiving or giving advice, flawed logic and limited information complicate the process. Advice seekers must identify their blind spots, recognize when and how to ask for guidance, draw useful insights from the right people, and overcome an inevitable defensiveness about their own views. Advisers, too, face myriad challenges as they try to interpret messy situations and provide guidance on seemingly intractable problems.

Below we describe the biggest obstacles on both sides. One reason they're so common is that they're basic—people often don't realize they're getting tripped up—so you may find it helpful to do a reality check of your behavior against these lists.

When you're seeking advice, watch for these obstacles:

Thinking you already have the answers.
As people are deciding whether they need help, they often have difficulty assessing their own competence and place too much

Idea in Brief

The Problem

Leaders must learn how to give and receive advice effectively to do their jobs well, but the exchange is hard work on both sides of the table. Doing it badly can lead to flawed decisions, strained relationships, and stalled careers.

The Solution

Fortunately, you can master the art of advice by adopting a framework of best practices, drawn from a substantial body of research.

The Benefits

By seeking advice from the right people—and in the right ways—you can develop smarter solutions to problems, deepen your thinking, and sharpen your decision making. And by becoming a better adviser, you'll extend your influence and learn from the people who come to you for guidance.

faith in their intuition. The result is overconfidence and a tendency to default to solo decision making on the basis of prior knowledge and assumptions. A related tendency is to ask for advice when one's real goal is to gain validation or praise. People do this when they strongly believe they've solved the problem but still want to "check the box" with bosses or peers. Or they do it when they have lurking doubts about a solution but dread the time and effort it would take to do better. It's a dangerous game to play—they risk alienating their advisers when it becomes evident (and it will) that they're requesting guidance just for show or to avoid additional work.

Choosing the wrong advisers.

Sometimes knowingly, sometimes not, decision makers stack the deck by turning to like-minded advisers. In a study of CEOs, for example, those at companies with poor financial performance (measured by market-to-book value) were more likely than those at high-performing ones to seek advice from executives in the same industry and with a similar functional background. The result was limited strategic change—less product-market and geographic diversification. What's more, several field studies confirm that advice seekers are more receptive to guidance from friends or other likable people.

Though friendship, accessibility, and nonthreatening personalities all impart high levels of comfort and trust, they have no relation to the quality or thoughtfulness of the advice.

Seekers also fail to think creatively enough about the expertise they need—which fields might bring valuable insight, who has solved a similar problem before, whose knowledge is most relevant, whose experience is the best fit—or cast a wide enough net to find it. Unfortunately, to make sense of a messy, volatile world, leaders often shoehorn people into tidy categories that don't reflect their full range of wisdom. That's a mistake President John F. Kennedy made leading up to the Bay of Pigs invasion. He didn't consult Secretary of Labor Arthur Goldberg for advice, assuming that Goldberg lacked a background in military matters. But as the journalist David Halberstam describes in *The Best and the Brightest*, Goldberg had run guerrilla operations during World War II, so he understood that guerrillas were "no good at all in confronting regular units." He explained to the president: "Whenever we used them like that, we'd always lose all our people. . . . But you didn't think of that—and you put me in the category of just a Secretary of Labor."

Defining the problem poorly.
Seekers frequently have trouble reaching a mutual understanding with their advisers—sometimes because of imprecise or ineffective communication, and sometimes because of cognitive or emotional blinders. When communicating ineffectively, they may tell a lengthy, blow-by-blow story that causes listeners to tune out, lose focus, and perhaps misidentify the core of the problem that needs solving. Or they may omit details that reflect badly on them but are central to seeing the big picture. Many seekers also take for granted background essentials (often about past incidents or organizational politics) that their advisers don't know. Or they may misdefine the problem by placing arbitrary boundaries around it and excluding important data, which skews their own and their advisers' assessments (a pitfall that the decision-making experts Max Bazerman and Dolly Chugh call *bounded awareness*).

Know what's called for

By understanding the different types of advice, seekers can make requests with greater precision—and advisers can give more-targeted guidance. We present the types separately here for clarity, but they frequently overlap in practice. For instance, one-off requests for guidance often segue into requests for counsel. And we've included coaching and mentoring, even though they aren't discussed in the chapter, in order to round out the picture of advice seeking and giving.

Type	Activities	Desired outcomes	Examples
Discrete advice	Exploring options for a single decision	Recommendations in favor of or against specific options	Which of my managers should I promote? Where should we build the new factory—in China, Brazil, or Eastern Europe?
Counsel	Providing guidance on how to approach a complex or unfamiliar situation	A framework or process for understanding and navigating the situation	How should I approach price negotiations with our overseas supplier? How should I handle my domineering supervisor?
Coaching	Enhancing skills, self-awareness, and self-management	Task proficiency; personal and professional development	How can I run more-effective meetings? How can I work more collaboratively with peers?
Mentoring	Providing opportunities, guidance, and protection to aid career success	A relationship dedicated to building and sustaining professional and personal effectiveness and to career advancement	Should I accept the position in Mumbai? How can I get more exposure for my project?

Discounting advice.

Once seekers have advice in hand, their most common mistake is to undervalue or dismiss it. This is a strong, recurrent finding in organizational behavior research—so it's pretty safe to assume that you're at least susceptible to this problem. For one thing, "egocentric bias" often clouds seekers' vision—even when people lack expertise, they put more stock in their own opinions than in others' views. For another, seekers understand their own logic but may be unaware of advisers' reasoning. Or they may become so anchored in their preformed judgments that they can't adjust their thinking when they receive feedback to the contrary. Over time, discounting advice can damage important relationships. Advisers notice when they're repeatedly not being heard, and it generates mistrust and ill will.

Individuals in powerful positions are the worst offenders. According to one experimental study, they feel competitive when they receive advice from experts, which inflates their confidence and leads them to dismiss what the experts are telling them. High-power participants in the study ignored almost two-thirds of the advice they received. Other participants (the control and low-power groups) ignored advice about half as often.

Misjudging the quality of advice.

Most seekers who accept advice have trouble distinguishing the good from the bad. Research shows that they value advice more if it comes from a confident source, even though confidence doesn't signal validity. Conversely, seekers tend to assume that advice is off-base when it veers from the norm or comes from people with whom they've had frequent discord. (Experimental studies show that neither indicates poor quality.) Seekers also don't embrace advice when advisers disagree among themselves. And they fail to compensate sufficiently for distorted advice that stems from conflicts of interest, even when their advisers have acknowledged the conflicts and the potential for self-serving motives.

When you're giving advice, be on the lookout for these tendencies:

Overstepping boundaries.

Though many people give unsolicited advice, it's usually considered intrusive and seldom followed. (That stands to reason. We all know what it's like to be on the receiving end of "helpful suggestions" we haven't invited and don't really want.) Another way advisers overstep is to chime in when they're not qualified to do so. It can give them an ego boost in the short run—but at a significant cost. People who liberally offer baseless advice quickly lose credibility and influence in their organizations. Even a single instance of bad advice normally leads to a rapid decline in an adviser's standing.

Misdiagnosing the problem.

Advisers must gather intelligence to develop a clearer picture of the problem to be solved. Here they can slip up in a couple of ways, as Edgar Schein, of MIT's Sloan School, has pointed out. First, they may define the problem prematurely because they *think* they see similarities with challenges they've faced. (Often those analogies don't hold up when the full scope of the problem is revealed.) Second, they sometimes forget that seekers are self-interested parties who may—deliberately or not—present partial or biased accounts. Taking such accounts at face value leads to inaccurate assessments and flawed advice. All this is compounded by an irrational but compelling fear of looking incompetent: Advisers tend to avoid asking basic, probing questions because they don't want to jeopardize their expert status.

Offering self-centered guidance.

Advisers often frame their guidance as "how I would respond if I were in your shoes." This approach is both off-putting and ineffective, because they're clearly not thinking about how the seeker feels, perceives the situation, and understands the choices ahead—the kinds of insights that lead to empathic understanding and useful recommendations. Advisers may also share personal stories and experiences that fail the "doability test" because they simply don't accord with the seeker's level of power, negotiating skill, organizational savvy, or situational constraints.

Advice on Advising

WILLIAM LEE is one of the foremost intellectual property attorneys in the United States, a former co-managing partner at WilmerHale, and the senior fellow of the Harvard Corporation, Harvard University's governing board, so he gives a lot of advice for a living. Because he's earned a reputation for doing it so skillfully, Garvin and Margolis included him in their research sample for this article. HBR spoke with Lee about his approach to advising and what he's learned with experience.

HBR: How would you describe your advising style?

Lee: I try to understand what the other person faces and provide guidance that makes sense from that perspective. My firm represents large clients such as Apple and Intel, but when we're advising institutions like that, we're also advising individuals who work there. They have the company's best interests in mind, but they have a boss to think about, their own goals, their personal lives, their ups and downs. Our advice has to work for them as well as for the institution. If we have something to say that the client CEO won't want to hear, we take the heat. If we're saying exactly what everyone wants to hear, we let an inside person report that.

How do you approach less formal advising—for instance, when you're mentoring someone?

Mentoring is the most important kind of advising, in my view. You have to really get to know the person. I like to begin with a simple, open-ended question: "How are things?" That lets you know what's on the other person's mind, so you can better understand what the issue is and how you might help.

What do you look for in an adviser?

Someone who is open and candid. Someone who gives advice that people can act on. (Otherwise it's like telling them, "Get taller" or "Get smarter.") Also,

Communicating advice poorly.

Several mistakes fall under this rubric. Advisers may provide vague recommendations that can easily be misconstrued. (For example, "Align behaviors with goals" might refer to unit goals or company goals, and it's not at all clear what behaviors are in question.) Or, when providing specialized expertise, they may use jargon or other inaccessible language. They may also overwhelm seekers with too many ideas, alternatives, action plans, perspectives, someone who recognizes that every situation is different. I advise clients. I also advise folks about their careers. A lot depends on the circumstances a person faces. When I was younger, and often on the receiving end, I was probably more inclined to believe that there's one way to think about problems. Over time I've realized it's more complicated than that. I've learned how important listening is.

Listening is a big theme in this article—but how do you home in on the right details?

At times the conversation has to be guided. Asking "Have you thought of the issue this way?" or "How would so-and-so think about the problem?" can turn the conversation in a different direction. The hardest thing to resist is simply cutting off a wandering narrative and giving the advice. It's much better to ask questions that allow people to reach conclusions themselves. If they do, they'll feel much more confident in the process and the choices they make.

What were some of your toughest experiences?

About 25 years ago I was the lead trial lawyer in a major case. My second chair was younger, a fine lawyer and a great person. We worked well together. When he came up for partner, we both knew that the decision was largely up to me. He had great presence, but his skills weren't the best match for the direction the firm was headed. Over lunch one day, we talked openly about it. I told him he'd be enormously successful in a different environment, but not if he stayed with the firm. He went somewhere else and really thrived there. It was the most difficult conversation I've ever had at work, and he later told me the same. But he also said it was the best conversation he's ever had.

or interpretations. Nothing causes paralysis like a laundry list of options with no explicit guidance on where to start or how to work through and winnow the list.

Mishandling the aftermath.
Though the final decision is not theirs to make, many advisers take offense when their guidance isn't accepted wholesale, curtailing further discussion. This has both short- and long-term costs: in the

moment, lost opportunities to provide a general sense of direction even if some of the seeker's choices are not to their liking; and over time, a growing distance between adviser and seeker that may limit the trust and intimacy that lie at the heart of effective advising. The reality is that recipients rarely take one person's advice and run with it. More often they modify the advice, combine it with feedback from others, or reject it altogether—and advisers often fail to treat these responses as valuable input in an ongoing conversation.

Best Practices for Seeking and Giving Advice

As a leader and a decision maker, you must "give as good as you get," and vice versa—but how can you overcome all those obstacles? We've identified some guidelines by combining lessons from academic research with the practical wisdom of experts on the ground—people we interviewed because they are known for their skill at advising. Although they come from a variety of fields (technology, financial services, law, politics, educational administration, consulting, and not for profit), we found striking parallels in their behavior throughout the five stages of advising. (See the sidebar "Guidelines for Each Stage of Advising.")

Stage 1: Finding the right fit.

Each request for advice is unique, reflecting a distinctive combination of circumstances, personalities, and events. But because time is often of the essence, you won't want to search anew for potential advisers in every situation. Put together a personal "board" in advance, including people you value not only for their judgment and their ability to keep confidences but also for their diverse strengths, experiences, and points of view. All of them should have your best interests at heart and a track record of being *really* willing to tell you what you don't want to hear. Try to find at least one person you can turn to in a variety of situations, because that adviser will develop a multifaceted sense of the problems you face and your natural proclivities and biases.

When selecting an adviser (or multiple advisers) from that board for your immediate needs, determine how you'd like her to help and why. (See the sidebar "What Advisers Can Do.") Sometimes you'll want a sounding board—someone who can listen carefully to help clarify and sharpen your thinking. At other times you'll want to test a path or an alternative you've tentatively chosen. Or you may want someone who can expand your frame of reference, drawing on rich experience and expertise to unveil dimensions of the problem that you did not see. Or perhaps you're looking for process guidance—a way of navigating through a ticklish situation—or help generating substantive ideas. The better you understand what you need, the better your selection will be—and the better equipped your adviser will be to support you.

Take this example: A regional supply chain head at a medical supply company was asked by the chief procurement officer to play hardball with a local government that was perpetually late paying for purchases. As the accounts receivable kept stacking up, the CPO suggested choking off supply—but the manager worried that government officials would turn that into a cause célèbre. It was a high-stakes situation, and he needed guidance. When considering potential advisers, he knew he wanted people who could provide calibration. Were his concerns justified or blown out of proportion? The person with the most-relevant experience, he decided, was a manager who oversaw supply chain in a similarly sensitive region. He also turned to a colleague with experience analyzing risks across borders. As a result, he was able to make a balanced recommendation to the CPO: that they canvass multiple regional heads about his proposed plan to choke off supply. And on the basis of their input, the CPO decided not to move ahead with his plan.

As the supply chain manager realized, no single adviser can be helpful in all situations, and the most readily accessible one might not be the right fit. Try to pinpoint what you don't know and how that accords with the knowledge and experiences of the people you might turn to. As the Harvard Business School professor C. Roland Christensen frequently observed, "When you pick your advisers, you pick your advice." Your goal is to find a match between your deficiencies, limitations, or uncertainties and their experiences, expertise, or knowledge base. Avoid picking advisers primarily for their

Guidelines for Each Stage of Advising

Stage 1: Finding the Right Fit

If You're a Seeker . . .

- Have a preexisting "board" of diverse, complementary advisers
- Determine what type of advice you are seeking
- Choose one or more advisers who fit your current needs

If You're an Adviser . . .

- Assess fit: Do you have the time, expertise, and experience to help?
- Identify other potential sources of guidance

Stage 2: Developing a Shared Understanding

If You're a Seeker . . .

- Provide just enough information about your problem
- Acknowledge uncomfortable truths

If You're an Adviser . . .

- Set the stage for effective advising: Allow ample time, and choose a place that's free from distractions and ensures privacy
- Listen actively and suspend judgment
- Ask open-ended questions to broaden understanding and then shift to more-detailed probes
- Once you have a complete picture of the problem, agree on what type of advice is needed

Stage 3: Crafting Alternatives

If You're a Seeker . . .

- Contribute actively to the development of options
- Ask questions to understand:
  - the costs, benefits, and rationale of each option

- the relevance and applicability of the advice
- the approach to implementation

If You're an Adviser . . .

- Understand and articulate your role as providing guidance, not making the decision
- Push to generate several viable choices
- Spell out the rationale, personal experiences, and principles behind your advice

Stage 4: Converging on a Decision

If You're a Seeker . . .

- Beware of uncritical and dismissive reflexes
- Consider soliciting a second or third opinion
- Develop hybrid solutions

If You're an Adviser . . .

- Ensure that all the options are evaluated; don't jump too quickly to a solution
- Pause frequently for reactions
- Convey your availability for further clarification and elaboration

Stage 5: Putting Advice into Action

If You're a Seeker . . .

- Be sensitive to changes in the situation or context and any need for midcourse corrections
- Follow up and seek additional guidance if necessary

If You're an Adviser

- Reaffirm that the decision and the consequences are the seeker's
- Convey your availability for additional guidance and support

confidence, likability, friendship, or reinforcing points of view—as noted earlier, those are not proxies for quality.

When the roles are reversed and you're approached for advice, ask yourself whether you are indeed a good fit. Do you have the right background to help in this particular situation? Can you dedicate enough time and effort to attend to the seeker's concerns? It's much better to decline the request than to give uninformed advice, rush the advisee, be distracted in meetings, or discover late in the process that you have little of value to offer. Ask why the advisee sought you out—but remember that *you* are in the best position to assess whether your judgment and experience are relevant. Saying no is a service too, and you can further help by identifying other sources of expertise. Even if you are well qualified to serve as an adviser, consider recommending some other people to bring in complementary or alternative views. That will give the seeker a more textured understanding of the challenges and choices.

Stage 2: Developing a shared understanding.

At this stage your primary goal as an advice seeker is to convey *just enough* information for your adviser to grasp the problem you face, why it poses a challenge, and where you hope to end up. That will allow her to offer informed, unbiased recommendations without getting lost in the weeds. So ground your narrative with telling details and provide context—but avoid taking her on a lengthy tour of antecedents, diverse interpretations, and potential consequences. Otherwise you may distract her from the central issues or lose her interest.

In the telling, you may need to acknowledge some uncomfortable truths about your behavior or weaknesses. Your discomfort with revealing certain information may actually signal its importance to fleshing out the story. An adviser can be only as good as the personal and organizational portrait she has to work with, so share all key details—even those that are unflattering or difficult to discuss. It will help her get past your biases and blind spots.

As an adviser, you'll want to get a complete picture while also expanding the seeker's understanding, all in a reasonable amount

What advisers can do

Depending on what's needed, advisers might:

Serve as a sounding board	Test a tentative path	Expand the frame of reference	Provide process guidance	Generate substantive ideas
Restate and play back arguments to sharpen the seeker's understanding of the situation and the conclusions she has drawn	Scrutinize the reasoning behind the selection of an option and elaborate on the potential consequence	Provide greater breadth and depth of understanding about the nature of the problem the seeker faces—and the implication for action	Suggest how to approach and manage a complicated, delicate, or high-stakes situation	Increase the number and range of options being considered

KEY PRACTICES

Asking a few well-chosen questions that probe the seekers' underlying rationale and motivation— and listening attentively	Assessing the seeker's thinking, often using hypotheticals and critical questions to achieve a deeper understanding	Sharing key details and tendencies from prior experiences in similar situations to flesh out the larger context	Examining the interests involved, the possibilities for action, and alternative steps the seeker might take	Brainstorming with the seeker

of time. So set the stage for openness and efficiency: Pick a place that will free you both from distractions and allow sufficient (but not unlimited) time for a robust discussion. Privacy and confidentiality are essential. Create a "safe zone" where you can both speak openly. Hear the seeker out, allowing his story to emerge with minimal intervention. Suspend judgment and resist the urge to provide immediate feedback and direction: You don't yet know enough to offer thoughtful advice. Jumping to conclusions or recommendations typically signals a flawed or incomplete diagnosis, so gather more information. Begin with broad, open-ended questions—such as "How are you feeling about this?"—because they establish rapport, uncover what is truly on the seeker's mind, and often take you right to the heart of the matter. (Anthropologists call these "grand tour questions" and suggest using them as a starting point for interviews.) Follow up by drawing out supporting details and additional context to help the seeker move beyond a self-serving account.

In our interviews with advisers, two people shared stories about seekers who had come to them for affirmation, already intent on a course of action. Both seekers had (and thus articulated) only a partial view of the problem; the advisers said they had to tease out the rest through patient inquiry before they could begin to formulate sound advice and move the seekers from affirmation mode to a dawning and genuine understanding of the challenges they faced.

Determine the seeker's personal interests and goals and compare them with those of the organization. Consider, in the words of one of our experts, giving "homework assignments" to further the seeker's thinking ("Come back to me next week with five reasons why moving to Dallas would be a good idea"). Finally, deepen your own understanding as well, by inquiring about root causes, potential consequences, and other pertinent issues not explicitly mentioned. They'll speak volumes if you can get them out in the open. The stated problem may be only a symptom of these underlying issues.

Once you've done all that, you'll be well enough informed to agree or disagree with the seeker on a key question that is seldom asked: What role should you play? Should you serve as a sounding board, provide reassurance, flesh out the picture the seeker has of this sort of situation, or present fresh insights and options? Discuss your conclusions with your advisee to ensure a shared understanding of what's needed.

Stage 3: Crafting alternatives.
Because decision making improves dramatically when diverse options are available, seekers and advisers should work together to come up with more than one possibility. Even go/no-go decisions yield improved results when nuanced alternatives are described and considered.

Take this example from our interviews: A consumer products division head at an electronics company decided to relocate his marketing group to improve collaboration with engineering. He was eager to adopt this industry trend because of its potential to speed up product development and get everyone thinking about more-targeted offerings. But his marketing VP felt it would put too much distance between her staff and sales.

So the division head turned to a trusted colleague, the chief operating officer, for advice on how to deal with marketing. The COO agreed that the move made sense and worked with the division head to generate ideas for getting the marketing VP on board—without resorting to fiat. For instance, the division head might try sharing the proposal at small cross-functional meetings so that the VP could hear her direct reports discuss the merits of being closer to the engineers. They could also meet with major retail customers or Wall Street analysts—either could comment on how competitors were benefiting from this approach. Talking to the COO expanded the division head's perspective—he could now see options beyond one-on-one conversations with the VP.

If you're seeking advice, adopt an analytic, probing mindset to identify and weigh multiple choices. Certainly offer up your own ideas, but also listen to your adviser's suggestions, especially those that may take you in a different direction altogether. Imagine how you might apply those recommendations—but subject them to a lot of poking and prodding as well. You want to play out what you would actually do. Ask pointed questions about the costs and benefits of each, the underlying rationale, the relevance of the advice to your situation (to confirm that your adviser isn't forcing his preferred principles and prior experiences to fit), the tactics for implementing the ideas, what repercussions might follow, and any contingencies you should prepare for. In short, scrutinize the advice as closely as your adviser scrutinized your description of the problem to be solved. The ensuing discussion will prepare you to overcome implementation hurdles.

If you're the adviser, think of yourself as a driving instructor. While you provide oversight and guidance, your ultimate goal is to empower the seeker to act independently. Our interviewees were unanimous in saying, essentially, "It's the seeker's job to find the path forward." You can never fully step into the advisee's shoes, and it is important to acknowledge that clearly. As you're helping her generate viable choices, spell out the thinking behind each possibility. Describe the principles that are shaping your advice, along with any experiences you are bringing to bear or using as analogies. Articulating your thought process—and your possible biases—can help both you and the seeker determine how well your reasoning and perspective fit the situation. If you are senior to the seeker, you can shrink the power difference and increase the likelihood that your advice will be useful by explicitly asking what doesn't seem quite right.

Stage 4: Converging on a decision.

When it's time to narrow down options and choose a course of action, seekers often fall prey to confirmation bias, picking the "easy way out," or other forms of flawed reasoning. So test your thinking by reviewing discarded or briefly considered options and by asking your adviser to play devil's advocate. And don't hesitate to solicit a second or third opinion at this stage—particularly if you remain uncertain. This can offset any biases or conflicts of interest your adviser may have. Experimental evidence suggests that two opinions are generally enough to yield most of the benefits of having multiple advisers. But for complex, ambiguous, highly visible, or contested problems, or when implementation is likely to be complicated, a few additional points of view are often helpful. No matter how unsettling or urgent the situation, resist the impulse to jump on the simplest, most readily available solution.

You may want to combine recommendations from multiple advisers with your own insights to form a hybrid solution. A team leader at a consulting firm did this when she was having a hard time managing project meetings. Veterans and newcomers would engage in endless debate, each faction convinced that the other didn't "get it." Because the leader communicated well with everybody one-on-

one, she considered reducing the group meetings and managing the project in hub-and-spoke fashion.

Her advisers provided a range of reactions. One emphasized the importance of allowing the group to discuss the client's challenges rather than just argue about competing solutions. Another said that the two camps needed to hear each other to broaden their perspectives. And a third suggested openly discussing the team's dysfunction. The leader drew on all three pieces of advice. After explaining in a series of one-on-ones how the next project meeting would be run and why, she brought her team together and asked individuals with varying levels of expertise and experience to share their views of the client's challenges. Debate didn't disappear, but it was far more constructive: Team members arrived at a collective understanding of the problems to be solved. At the end they talked about how they might have more meetings like that one.

If you're an adviser, your goal at this stage is to work with the advisee to explore all the options at hand before she makes a choice. Talk through the most likely outcomes of each possibility, assessing the relative pros and cons and ensuring that the conversation remains a dialogue rather than a monologue. Pose hypotheticals—"Imagine it's a year from now, and you did fire that talented but difficult manager. What might happen? How bad, or good, could things get?"—to tease out likely implications. Then focus the discussion on a course of action. This might entail making the case for a single option, or you might suggest experimenting with a few ideas.

Pause frequently to gauge how comfortable the seeker is with the proffered advice and the extent to which she accepts the underlying rationale. Work together to bring to the surface unstated assumptions, lingering doubts, and unresolved questions. At the same time, recognize that "I don't know" is a fine answer if you can't predict the impact of certain options, especially if you make clear recommendations on how to learn more about the alternatives.

Follow-up meetings are often essential for firming up advisees' choices and developing detailed action plans. So make yourself available for clarification and elaboration. That said, seekers sometimes come back for more and more conversations to delay decision making. If you suspect that's happening, either say so and ask what might be done to move things forward, or encourage the seeker to try out a solution and check in with you about how it went.

Stage 5: Putting advice into action.
As a seeker, you'll need to act on the advice you've received and make real-time adjustments. Advice is best treated as provisional and contingent: It should be a cycle of guidance, action, learning, and further guidance—not a fixed path forward. Especially if the advisory process has occurred over an extended period, circumstances may have changed by the time you are ready to act.

So follow up for further advice if needed. You may benefit from multiple meetings, especially if you have gleaned new information from your first steps forward or have a series of decisions to make. It's also considerate and helpful to let your adviser know what you've done and how it's working out. It's a way of expressing your gratitude, strengthening the relationship, and helping the adviser learn as well.

If you're the adviser, step back from the process at this stage. Reaffirm that it's up to the seeker to move forward. Both the decision and the consequences are his, not yours, and must be recognized as such. That will help ensure personal accountability and prevent misplaced blame if things don't work out as hoped. But remain open to providing additional guidance as events unfold. Especially in fluid, rapidly changing situations, even the best advice can quickly become irrelevant. To the extent that you're willing to help with midcourse corrections, convey your availability.

Though seekers and advisers work together to solve problems, they have different vantage points. Recent social psychology research shows that people in an advisory role focus on overarching purpose (*why* an action should be performed), whereas recipients of advice—who usually face an impending decision—are more concerned with tactics (*how* to get things done). An individual is likely to think idealistically as an adviser but pragmatically as a seeker, even when confronting the same challenge.

Suppose a hiring manager must decide whether to fill a key role with an outside candidate or promote an ambitious employee from within. If you're advising that manager, you may see the merits of bringing in a fresh perspective and the healthy shake-up it could provide. But if you're the one seeking guidance, you may be more inclined to see the challenges of getting an outsider integrated and poised to deliver and also the time saved and the boost to morale of going with an insider. Keeping both perspectives in mind, no matter which is yours, will help you achieve mutual understanding, identify the key priority driving the decision (reducing time and effort to integrate? bringing in a fresh perspective?), and prepare for the downsides of any option.

Overall, our guidelines for both seekers and advisers amount to a fundamental shift in approach. Although people typically focus on the content of advice, those who are most skilled attend just as much to *how* they advise as to *what* they advise. It's a mistake to think of advice as a one-and-done transaction. Skilled advising is more than the dispensing and accepting of wisdom; it's a creative, collaborative process—a matter of striving, on both sides, to better understand problems and craft promising paths forward. And that often requires an ongoing conversation.

Originally published in January–February 2015. Reprint R1501D

Find the Coaching in Criticism

by Sheila Heen and Douglas Stone

FEEDBACK IS CRUCIAL. That's obvious: It improves performance, develops talent, aligns expectations, solves problems, guides promotion and pay, and boosts the bottom line.

But it's equally obvious that in many organizations, feedback doesn't work. A glance at the stats tells the story: Only 36% of managers complete appraisals thoroughly and on time. In one recent survey, 55% of employees said their most recent performance review had been unfair or inaccurate, and one in four said they dread such evaluations more than anything else in their working lives. When senior HR executives were asked about their biggest performance management challenge, 63% cited managers' inability or unwillingness to have difficult feedback discussions. Coaching and mentoring? Uneven at best.

Most companies try to address these problems by training leaders to give feedback more effectively and more often. That's fine as far as it goes; everyone benefits when managers are better communicators. But improving the skills of the feedback giver won't accomplish much if the receiver isn't able to absorb what is said. It is the receiver who controls whether feedback is let in or kept out, who has to make sense of what he or she is hearing, and who decides whether or not to change. People need to stop treating feedback only as something that must be pushed and instead improve their ability to pull.

For the past 20 years we've coached executives on difficult conversations, and we've found that almost everyone, from new hires to C-suite veterans, struggles with receiving feedback. A critical performance review, a well-intended suggestion, or an oblique comment that may or may not even be feedback ("Well, your presentation was certainly interesting") can spark an emotional reaction, inject tension into the relationship, and bring communication to a halt. But there's good news, too: The skills needed to receive feedback well are distinct and learnable. They include being able to identify and manage the emotions triggered by the feedback and extract value from criticism even when it's poorly delivered.

Why Feedback Doesn't Register

What makes receiving feedback so hard? The process strikes at the tension between two core human needs—the need to learn and grow, and the need to be accepted just the way you are. As a result, even a seemingly benign suggestion can leave you feeling angry, anxious, badly treated, or profoundly threatened. A hedge such as "Don't take this personally" does nothing to soften the blow.

Getting better at receiving feedback starts with understanding and managing those feelings. You might think there are a thousand ways in which feedback can push your buttons, but in fact there are only three.

Truth triggers are set off by the content of the feedback. When assessments or advice seem off base, unhelpful, or simply untrue, you feel indignant, wronged, and exasperated.

Relationship triggers are tripped by the person providing the feedback. Exchanges are often colored by what you believe about the giver (He's got no credibility on this topic!) and how you feel about your previous interactions (After all I've done for you, I get this petty criticism?). So you might reject coaching that you would accept on its merits if it came from someone else.

Identity triggers are all about your relationship with yourself. Whether the feedback is right or wrong, wise or witless, it can be devastating if it causes your sense of who you are to come undone.

Idea in Brief

Feedback is crucial—but almost everyone, from new hires to C-suite executives, struggles with receiving it. The authors, who have spent 20 years working with managers on difficult conversations, outline six steps that can help you turn feedback into an important, and unthreatening, tool.

- **Know your tendencies.** Look for patterns in how you respond. Once you understand your standard operating procedure, you can make better choices about where to go from there.

- **Separate the "what" from the "who."** Your feelings about the messenger might be short-circuiting your ability to learn from the message.

- **Sort toward coaching.** Work to hear feedback as well-meant advice, not as an indictment.

- **Unpack the feedback.** Resist snap judgments; explore where suggestions are coming from and where they're going.

- **Request and direct feedback.** Don't wait for a formal review; ask for bite-size pieces of coaching.

- **Experiment.** Try following a piece of advice and seeing what happens.

Criticism is never easy to take—but learning to pull value from it is essential to your development and success.

In such moments you'll struggle with feeling overwhelmed, defensive, or off balance.

All these responses are natural and reasonable; in some cases they are unavoidable. The solution isn't to pretend you don't have them. It's to recognize what's happening and learn how to derive benefit from feedback even when it sets off one or more of your triggers.

Six Steps to Becoming a Better Receiver

Taking feedback well is a process of sorting and filtering. You need to understand the other person's point of view, try on ideas that may at first seem a poor fit, and experiment with different ways of doing things. You also need to discard or shelve critiques that are genuinely misdirected or are not helpful right away. But it's nearly impossible to do any of those things from inside a triggered response. Instead of ushering you into a nuanced conversation that will help you learn, your triggers prime you to reject, counterattack, or withdraw.

The six steps below will keep you from throwing valuable feedback onto the discard pile or—just as damaging—accepting and acting on comments that you would be better off disregarding. They are presented as advice to the receiver. But, of course, understanding the challenges of receiving feedback helps the giver to be more effective too.

1. Know your tendencies.

You've been getting feedback all your life, so there are no doubt patterns in how you respond. Do you defend yourself on the facts ("This is plain wrong"), argue about the method of delivery ("You're really doing this by e-mail?"), or strike back ("You, of all people?")? Do you smile on the outside but seethe on the inside? Do you get teary or filled with righteous indignation? And what role does the passage of time play? Do you tend to reject feedback in the moment and then step back and consider it over time? Do you accept it all immediately but later decide it's not valid? Do you agree with it intellectually but have trouble changing your behavior?

When Michael, an advertising executive, hears his boss make an offhand joke about his lack of professionalism, it hits him like a sledgehammer. "I'm flooded with shame," he told us, "and all my failings rush to mind, as if I'm Googling 'things wrong with me' and getting 1.2 million hits, with sponsored ads from my father and my ex. In this state it's hard to see the feedback at 'actual size.'" But now that Michael understands his standard operating procedure, he's able to make better choices about where to go from there: "I can reassure myself that I'm exaggerating, and usually after I sleep on it, I'm in a better place to figure out whether there's something I can learn."

2. Disentangle the "what" from the "who."

If the feedback is on target and the advice is wise, it shouldn't matter who delivers it. But it does. When a relationship trigger is activated, entwining the content of comments with your feelings about the giver (or about how, when, or where she delivered the comments), learning is short-circuited. To keep that from happening, you have to work to separate the message from the messenger and then consider both.

Janet, a chemist and a team leader at a pharmaceutical company, received glowing comments from her peers and superiors during her 360-degree review but was surprised by the negative feedback she got from her direct reports. She immediately concluded that the problem was theirs: "I have high standards, and some of them can't handle that," she remembers thinking. "They aren't used to someone holding their feet to the fire." In this way, she changed the subject from her management style to her subordinates' competence, preventing her from learning something important about the impact she had on others.

Eventually the penny dropped, Janet says. "I came to see that whether it was their performance problem or my leadership problem, those were not mutually exclusive issues, and both were worth solving." She was able to disentangle the issues and talk to her team about both. Wisely, she began the conversation with their feedback to her, asking, "What am I doing that's making things tough? What would improve the situation?"

3. Sort toward coaching.

Some feedback is evaluative ("Your rating is a 4"); some is coaching ("Here's how you can improve"). Everyone needs both. Evaluations tell you where you stand, what to expect, and what is expected of you. Coaching allows you to learn and improve and helps you play at a higher level.

It's not always easy to distinguish one from the other. When a board member phoned James to suggest that he start the next quarter's CFO presentation with analyst predictions rather than internal projections, was that intended as a helpful suggestion, or was it a veiled criticism of his usual approach? When in doubt, people tend to assume the worst and to put even well-intentioned coaching into the evaluation bin. Feeling judged is likely to set off your identity triggers, and the resulting anxiety can drown out the opportunity to learn. So whenever possible, sort toward coaching. Work to hear feedback as potentially valuable advice from a fresh perspective rather than as an indictment of how you've done things in the past. When James took that approach, "the suggestion became less emotionally loaded," he says. "I decided to hear it as simply an indication of how that board member might more easily digest quarterly information."

4. Unpack the feedback.
Often it's not immediately clear whether feedback is valid and useful. So before you accept or reject it, do some analysis to better understand it.

Here's a hypothetical example. Kara, who's in sales, is told by Johann, an experienced colleague, that she needs to "be more assertive." Her reaction might be to reject his advice ("I think I'm pretty assertive already"). Or she might acquiesce ("I really do need to step it up"). But before she decides what to do, she needs to understand what he really means. Does he think she should speak up more often, or just with greater conviction? Should she smile more, or less? Have the confidence to admit she doesn't know something, or the confidence to pretend she does?

Even the simple advice to "be more assertive" comes from a complex set of observations and judgments that Johann has made while watching Kara in meetings and with customers. Kara needs to dig into the general suggestion and find out what in particular prompted it. What did Johann see her do or fail to do? What did he expect, and what is he worried about? In other words, where is the feedback coming from?

Kara also needs to know where the feedback is going—exactly what Johann wants her to do differently and why. After a clarifying discussion, she might agree that she is less assertive than others on the sales floor but disagree with the idea that she should change. If all her sales heroes are quiet, humble, and deeply curious about customers' needs, Kara's view of what it means to be good at sales might look and sound very different from Johann's *Glengarry Glen Ross* ideal.

When you set aside snap judgments and take time to explore where feedback is coming from and where it's going, you can enter into a rich, informative conversation about perceived best practices—whether you decide to take the advice or not.

5. Ask for just one thing.

Feedback is less likely to set off your emotional triggers if you request it and direct it. So don't wait until your annual performance review. Find opportunities to get bite-size pieces of coaching from a variety of people throughout the year. Don't invite criticism with a big, unfocused question like "Do you have any feedback for me?" Make the process more manageable by asking a colleague, a boss, or a direct report, "What's one thing you see me doing (or failing to do) that holds me back?" That person may name the first behavior that comes to mind or the most important one on his or her list. Either way, you'll get concrete information and can tease out more specifics at your own pace.

Roberto, a fund manager at a financial services firm, found his 360-degree review process overwhelming and confusing. "Eighteen pages of charts and graphs and no ability to have follow-up conversations to clarify the feedback was frustrating," he says, adding that it also left him feeling awkward around his colleagues.

Now Roberto taps two or three people each quarter to ask for one thing he might work on. "They don't offer the same things, but over time I hear themes, and that gives me a good sense of where my growth edge lies," he says. "And I have really good conversations—with my boss, with my team, even with peers where there's some friction in the relationship. They're happy to tell me one thing to change, and often they're right. It does help us work more smoothly together."

Research has shown that those who explicitly seek critical feedback (that is, who are not just fishing for praise) tend to get higher performance ratings. Why? Mainly, we think, because someone who's asking for coaching is more likely to take what is said to heart and genuinely improve. But also because when you ask for feedback, you not only find out how others see you, you also *influence* how they see you. Soliciting constructive criticism communicates humility, respect, passion for excellence, and confidence, all in one go.

6. Engage in small experiments.

After you've worked to solicit and understand feedback, it may still be hard to discern which bits of advice will help you and which ones won't. We suggest designing small experiments to find out. Even though you may doubt that a suggestion will be useful, if the downside risk is small and the upside potential is large, it's worth a try. James, the CFO we discussed earlier, decided to take the board member's advice for the next presentation and see what happened. Some directors were pleased with the change, but the shift in format prompted others to offer suggestions of their own. Today James reverse-engineers his presentations to meet board members' current top-of-mind concerns. He sends out an e-mail a week beforehand asking for any burning questions, and either front-loads his talk with answers to them or signals at the start that he will get to them later on. "It's a little more challenging to prepare for but actually much easier to give," he says. "I spend less time fielding unexpected questions, which was the hardest part of the job."

That's an example worth following. When someone gives you advice, test it out. If it works, great. If it doesn't, you can try again, tweak your approach, or decide to end the experiment.

Criticism is never easy to take. Even when you know that it's essential to your development and you trust that the person delivering it wants you to succeed, it can activate psychological triggers. You might feel misjudged, ill-used, and sometimes threatened to your very core.

Your growth depends on your ability to pull value from criticism in spite of your natural responses and on your willingness to seek out even more advice and coaching from bosses, peers, and subordinates. They may be good or bad at providing it, or they may have little time for it—but you are the most important factor in your own development. If you're determined to learn from whatever feedback you get, no one can stop you.

Originally published in January–February 2014. R1401K

Visualizations That Really Work

by Scott Berinato

NOT LONG AGO, THE ABILITY to create smart data visualizations, or dataviz, was a nice-to-have skill. For the most part, it benefited design- and data-minded managers who made a deliberate decision to invest in acquiring it. That's changed. Now visual communication is a must-have skill for all managers, because more and more often, it's the only way to make sense of the work they do.

Data is the primary force behind this shift. Decision making increasingly relies on data, which comes at us with such overwhelming velocity, and in such volume, that we can't comprehend it without some layer of abstraction, such as a visual one. A typical example: At Boeing the managers of the Osprey program need to improve the efficiency of the aircraft's takeoffs and landings. But each time the Osprey gets off the ground or touches back down, its sensors create a terabyte of data. Ten takeoffs and landings produce as much data as is held in the Library of Congress. Without visualization, detecting the inefficiencies hidden in the patterns and anomalies of that data would be an impossible slog.

But even information that's not statistical demands visual expression. Complex systems—business process workflows, for example, or the way customers move through a store—are hard to understand, much less fix, if you can't first see them.

Thanks to the internet and a growing number of affordable tools, translating information into visuals is now easy (and cheap) for everyone, regardless of data skills or design skills. This is largely a positive development. One drawback, though, is that it reinforces the impulse to "click and viz" without first thinking about your purpose and goals. *Convenient* is a tempting replacement for good, but it will lead to charts that are merely adequate or, worse, ineffective. Automatically converting spreadsheet cells into a chart only visualizes pieces of a spreadsheet; it doesn't capture an idea. As the presentation expert Nancy Duarte puts it, "Don't project the idea that you're showing a chart. Project the idea that you're showing a reflection of human activity, of things people did to make a line go up and down. It's not 'Here are our Q3 financial results,' it's 'Here's where we missed our targets.'"

Managers who want to get better at making charts often start by learning rules. When should I use a bar chart? How many colors are too many? Where should the key go? Do I have to start my y-axis at zero? Visual grammar is important and useful—but knowing it doesn't guarantee that you'll make good charts. To start with chart-making rules is to forgo strategy for execution; it's to pack for a trip without knowing where you're going.

Your visual communication will prove far more successful if you begin by acknowledging that it is not a lone action but, rather, several activities, each of which requires distinct types of planning, resources, and skills. The typology I offer here was created as a reaction to my making the very mistake I just described: The book from which this article is adapted started out as something like a rule book. But after exploring the history of visualization, the exciting state of visualization research, and smart ideas from experts and pioneers, I reconsidered the project. We didn't need another rule book; we needed a way to think about the increasingly crucial discipline of visual communication as a whole.

The typology described in this article is simple. By answering just two questions, you can set yourself up to succeed.

The Two Questions

To start thinking visually, consider the nature and purpose of your visualization:

Idea in Brief

Context

Knowledge workers need greater visual literacy than they used to, because so much data—and so many ideas—are now presented graphically. But few of us have been taught data-visualization skills.

Tools Are Fine . . .

Inexpensive tools allow anyone to perform simple tasks such as importing spreadsheet data into a bar chart. But that means it's easy to create terrible charts. Visualization can be so much more: It's an agile, powerful way to explore ideas and communicate information.

. . . But Strategy Is Key

Don't jump straight to execution. Instead, first think about what you're representing—ideas or data? Then consider your purpose: Do you want to inform, persuade, or explore? The answers will suggest what tools and resources you need.

Is the information *conceptual* or *data-driven?*
Am I *declaring* something or *exploring* something?

If you know the answers to these questions, you can plan what resources and tools you'll need and begin to discern what type of visualization will help you achieve your goals most effectively.

	Conceptual	Data-driven
Focus	*Ideas*	*Statistics*
Goals	*Simplify, teach* "Here's how our organization is structured."	*Inform, enlighten* "Here are our revenues for the past two years."

The first question is the simpler of the two, and the answer is usually obvious. Either you're visualizing qualitative information or you're plotting quantitative information: ideas or statistics. But notice that the question is about the information itself, not the forms you might ultimately use to show it. For example, the classic Gartner Hype Cycle (see following page) uses a traditionally data-driven form—a line chart—but no actual data. It's a concept.

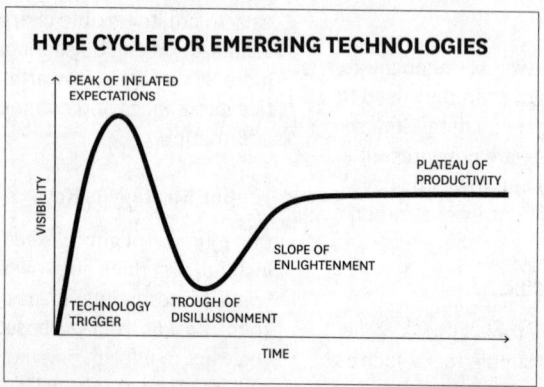

If the first question identifies what you *have,* the second elicits what you're *doing:* either communicating information (declarative) or trying to figure something out (exploratory).

	Declarative	Exploratory
Focus	*Documenting, designing*	*Prototyping, iterating, interacting, automating*
Goals	*Affirm* "Here is our budget by department."	*Confirm* "Let's see if marketing investments contributed to rising profits." *Discover* "What would we see if we visualized customer purchases by gender, location, and purchase amount in real time?"

Managers most often work with declarative visualizations, which make a statement, usually to an audience in a formal setting. If you have a spreadsheet workbook full of sales data and you're using it to show quarterly sales in a presentation, your purpose is declarative.

But let's say your boss wants to understand why the sales team's performance has lagged lately. You suspect that seasonal cycles have caused the dip, but you're not sure. Now your purpose is exploratory, and you'll use the same data to create visuals that will confirm or refute your hypothesis. The audience is usually yourself or a small team. If your hypothesis is confirmed, you may well show your boss a declarative visualization, saying, "Here's what's happening to sales."

Exploratory visualizations are actually of two kinds. In the example above, you were testing a hypothesis. But suppose you don't have an idea about why performance is lagging—you don't know what you're looking for. You want to mine your workbook to see what patterns, trends, and anomalies emerge. What will you see, for example, when you measure sales performance in relation to the size of the region a salesperson manages? What happens if you compare seasonal trends in various geographies? How does weather affect sales? Such data brainstorming can deliver fresh insights. Big strategic questions—Why are revenues falling? Where can we find efficiencies? How do customers interact with us?—can benefit from a discovery-focused exploratory visualization.

The Four Types

The nature and purpose questions combine in a classic 2×2 to define four types of visual communication: idea illustration, idea generation, visual discovery, and everyday dataviz.

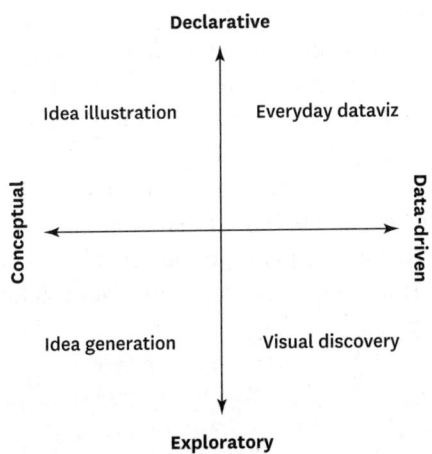

Idea illustration.

Info type	Process, framework
Typical setting	Presentations, teaching
Primary skills	Design, editing
Goals	Learning, simplifying, explaining

We might call this quadrant the "consultants' corner." Consultants can't resist process diagrams, cycle diagrams, and the like. At their best, idea illustrations clarify complex ideas by drawing on our ability to understand metaphors (trees, bridges) and simple design conventions (circles, hierarchies). Org charts and decision trees are classic examples of idea illustration. So is the 2×2 that frames this article.

Idea illustration demands clear and simple design, but its reliance on metaphor invites unnecessary adornment. Because the discipline and boundaries of data sets aren't built in to idea illustration, they must be imposed. The focus should be on clear communication, structure, and the logic of the ideas. The most useful skills here are similar to what a text editor brings to a manuscript—the ability to pare things down to their essence. Some design skills will be useful too, whether they're your own or hired.

Suppose a company engages consultants to help its R&D group find inspiration in other industries. The consultants use a technique called the *pyramid search*—a way to get information from experts in other fields close to your own, who point you to the top experts in their fields, who point you to experts in still other fields, who then help you find the experts in those fields, and so on.

It's actually tricky to explain, so the consultants may use visualization to help. How does a pyramid search work? It looks something like this:

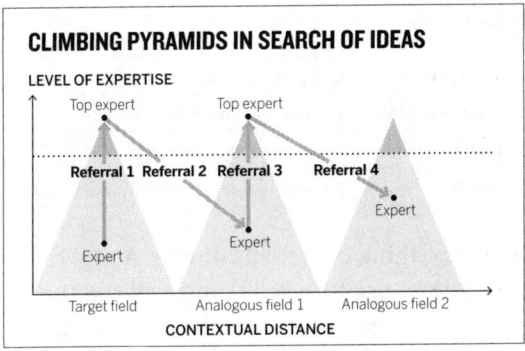

The axes use conventions that we can grasp immediately: industries plotted near to far and expertise mapped low to high. The pyramid shape itself shows the relative rarity of top experts compared with lower-level ones. Words in the title—"climbing" and "pyramids"—help us grasp the idea quickly. Finally, the designer didn't succumb to a temptation to decorate: The pyramids aren't literal, three-dimensional, sandstone-colored objects.

Too often, idea illustration doesn't go that well, and you end up with something like this:

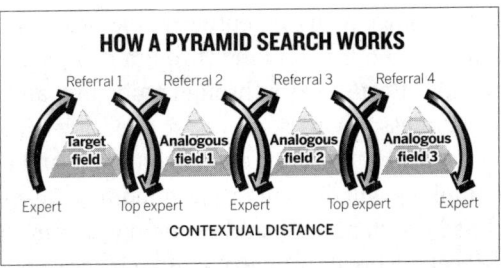

Here the color gradient, the drop shadows, and the 3-D pyramids distract us from the idea. The arrows don't actually demonstrate how a pyramid search works. And experts and top experts are placed on the same plane instead of at different heights to convey relative status.

Idea generation.

Info type	Complex, undefined
Typical setting	Working session, brainstorming
Primary skills	Team-building, facilitation
Goals	Problem-solving, discovery, innovation

Managers may not think of visualization as a tool to support idea generation, but they use it to brainstorm all the time—on whiteboards, on butcher paper, or, classically, on the back of a napkin. Like idea illustration, idea generation relies on conceptual metaphors, but it takes place in more-informal settings, such as off-sites, strategy sessions, and early-phase innovation projects. It's used to find new ways of seeing how the business works and to answer complex managerial challenges: restructuring an organization, coming up with a new business process, codifying a system for making decisions.

Although idea generation can be done alone, it benefits from collaboration and borrows from design thinking—gathering as many diverse points of view and visual approaches as possible before homing in on one and refining it. Jon Kolko, the founder and director of the Austin Center for Design and the author of *Well-Designed: How to Use Empathy to Create Products People Love,* fills the whiteboard walls of his office with conceptual, exploratory visualizations. "It's our go-to method for thinking through complexity," he says. "Sketching is this effort to work through ambiguity and muddiness and come to crispness." Managers who are good at leading teams, facilitating brainstorming sessions, and encouraging and then capturing creative thinking will do well in this quadrant. Design skills and editing are less important here, and sometimes counterproductive. When you're seeking breakthroughs, editing is the opposite of what you need, and you should think in rapid sketches; refined designs will just slow you down.

Suppose a marketing team is holding an off-site. The team members need to come up with a way to show executives their proposed strategy for going upmarket. An hour-long whiteboard session yields several approaches and ideas (none of which are erased) for presenting the strategy. Ultimately, one approach gains purchase with the team, which thinks it best captures the key point: Get fewer customers to spend much more. The whiteboard looks something like this:

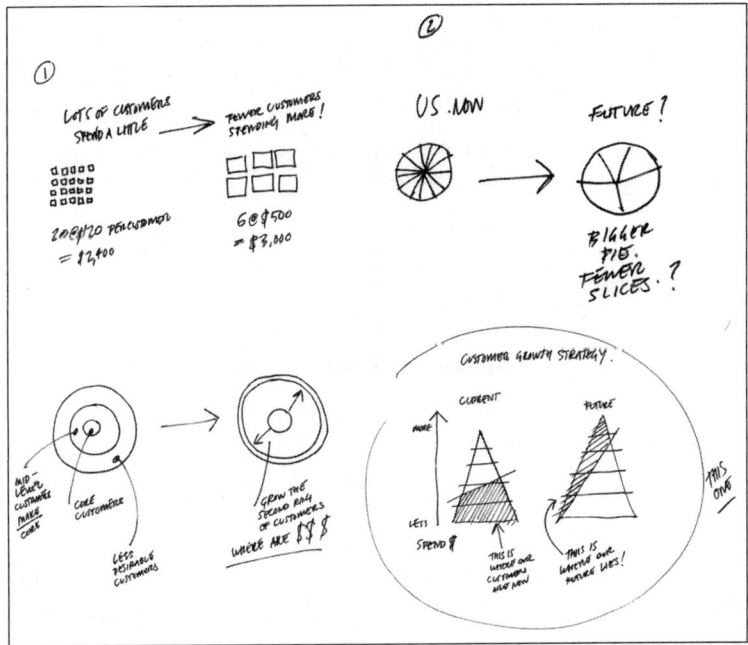

Of course, visuals that emerge from idea generation often lead to more formally designed and presented idea illustrations.

Visual discovery.

Info type	Big data, complex, dynamic
Typical setting	Working sessions, testing, analysis
Primary skills	Business intelligence, programming, paired analysis
Goals	Trend spotting, sense making, deep analysis

This is the most complicated quadrant, because in truth it holds two categories. Recall that we originally separated exploratory purposes into two kinds: testing a hypothesis and mining for patterns, trends, and anomalies. The former is focused, whereas the latter is more flexible. The bigger and more complex the data, and the less you know going in, the more open-ended the work.

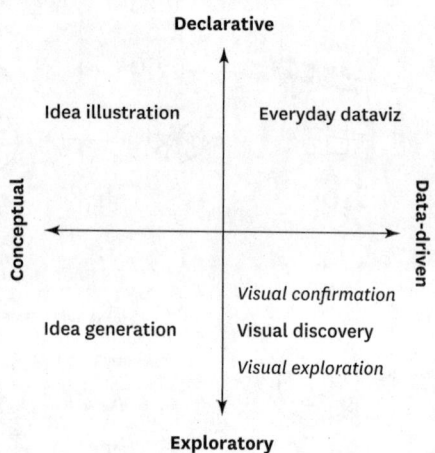

Visual confirmation. You're answering one of two questions with this kind of project: Is what I suspect actually true? or What are some other ways of depicting this idea?

The scope of the data tends to be manageable, and the chart types you're likely to use are common—although when trying to depict things in new ways, you may venture into some less-common types. Confirmation usually doesn't happen in a formal setting; it's the work you do to find the charts you want to create for presentations. That means your time will shift away from design and toward prototyping that allows you to rapidly iterate on the dataviz. Some skill at manipulating spreadsheets and knowledge of programs or sites that enable swift prototyping are useful here.

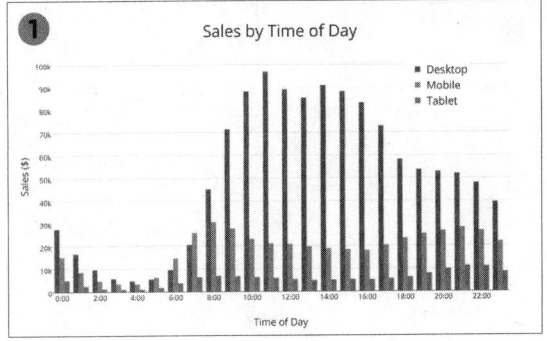

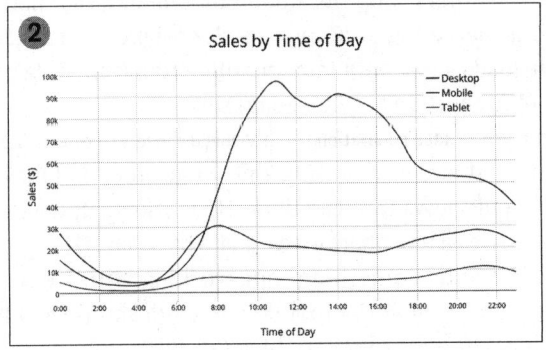

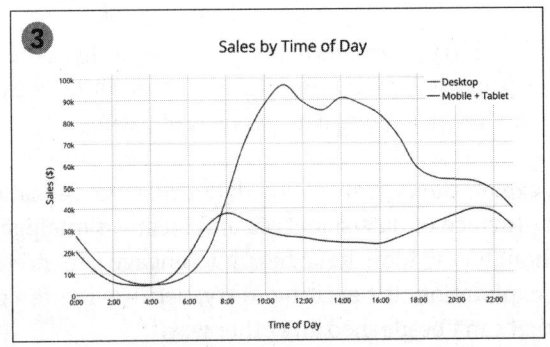

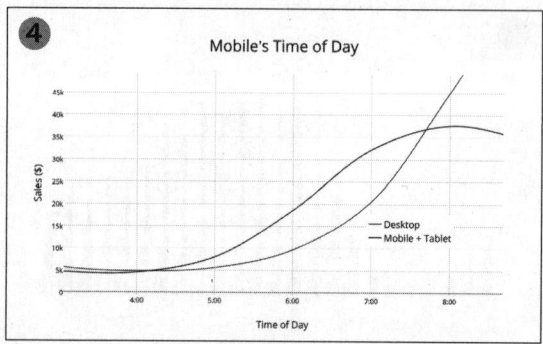

Suppose a marketing manager believes that at certain times of the day more customers shop his site on mobile devices than on desktops, but his marketing programs aren't designed to take advantage of that. He loads some data into an online tool (called Datawrapper) to see if he's right (1 on previous page).

He can't yet confirm or refute his hypothesis. He can't tell much of anything, but he's prototyping and using a tool that makes it easy to try different views into the data. He works fast; design is not a concern. He tries a line chart instead of a bar chart (2).

Now he's seeing something, but working with three variables still doesn't quite get at the mobile-versus-desktop view he wants, so he tries again with two variables (3). Each time he iterates, he evaluates whether he can confirm his original hypothesis: At certain times of day more customers are shopping on mobile devices than on desktops.

On the fourth try he zooms in and confirms his hypothesis (4).

New software tools mean this type of visualization is easier than ever before: They're making data analysts of us all.

Visual exploration. Open-ended data-driven visualizations tend to be the province of data scientists and business intelligence analysts, although new tools have begun to engage general managers in visual exploration. It's exciting to try, because it often produces insights that can't be gleaned any other way.

Because we don't know what we're looking for, these visuals tend to plot data more inclusively. In extreme cases, this kind of project may combine multiple data sets or load dynamic, real-time data into a system that updates automatically. Statistical modeling benefits from visual exploration.

Exploration also lends itself to interactivity: Managers can adjust parameters, inject new data sources, and continually revisualize. Complex data sometimes also suits specialized and unusual visualization, such as *force-directed diagrams* that show how networks cluster, or topographical plots.

Function trumps form here: Analytical, programming, data management, and business intelligence skills are more crucial than the ability to create presentable charts. Not surprisingly, this half of the quadrant is where managers are most likely to call in experts to help set up systems to wrangle data and create visualizations that fit their analytic goals.

Anmol Garg, a data scientist at Tesla Motors, has used visual exploration to tap into the vast amount of sensor data the company's cars produce. Garg created an interactive chart that shows the pressure in a car's tires over time. In true exploratory form, he and his team first created the visualizations and then found a variety of uses for them: to see whether tires are properly inflated when a car leaves the factory, how often customers reinflate them, and how long customers take to respond to a low-pressure alert; to find leak rates; and to do some predictive modeling on when tires are likely to go flat. The pressure of all four tires is visualized on a scatter plot, which, however inscrutable to a general audience, is clear to its intended audience.

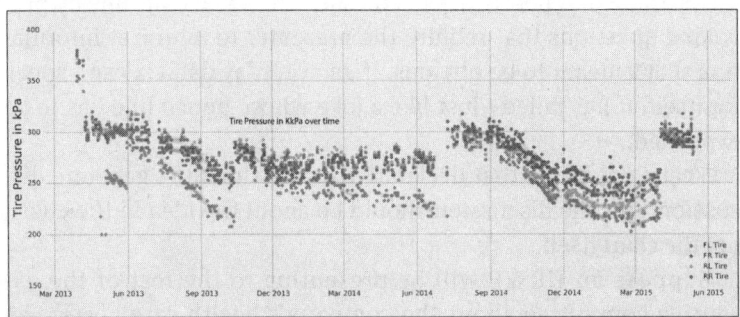

Garg was exploring data to find insights that could be gleaned only through visuals. "We're dealing with terabytes of data all the time," he says. "You can't find anything looking at spreadsheets and querying databases. It has to be visual." For presentations to the executive team, Garg translates these exploration sessions into the kinds of simpler charts discussed below. "Management loves seeing visualizations," he says.

Everyday dataviz.

Info type	Simple, low volume
Typical setting	Formal, presentations
Primary skills	Design, storytelling
Goals	Affirming, setting context

Whereas data scientists do most of the work on visual exploration, managers do most of the work on everyday visualizations. This quadrant comprises the basic charts and graphs you normally paste from a spreadsheet into a presentation. They are usually simple—line charts, bar charts, pies, and scatter plots.

"Simple" is the key. Ideally, the visualization will communicate a single message, charting only a few variables. And the goal is straightforward: affirming and setting context. Simplicity is primarily a design challenge, so design skills are important. Clarity and consistency make these charts most effective in the setting where they're typically used: a formal presentation. In a presentation, time is constrained. A poorly designed chart will waste that time by provoking questions that require the presenter to interpret information that's meant to be obvious. If an everyday dataviz can't speak for itself, it has failed—just like a joke whose punch line has to be explained.

That's not to say that declarative charts shouldn't generate discussion. But the discussion should be about the idea in the chart, not the chart itself.

Suppose an HR VP will be presenting to the rest of the executive committee about the company's health care costs. She wants to convey that the growth of these costs has slowed significantly, creating an opportunity to invest in additional health care services.

The VP has read an online report about this trend that includes a link to some government data. She downloads the data and clicks on the line chart option in Excel. She has her viz in a few seconds. But because this is for a presentation, she asks a designer colleague to add detail from the data set to give a more comprehensive view.

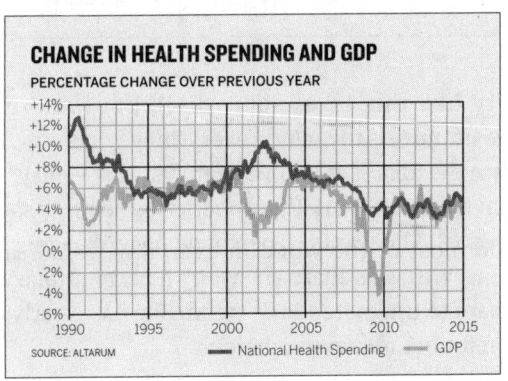

This is a well-designed, accurate chart, but it's probably not the right one. The executive committee doesn't need two decades' worth of historical context to discuss the company's strategy for employee benefits investments. The point the VP wants to make is that cost increases have slowed over the past few years. Is that clearly communicated here?

In general, when it takes more than a few seconds to digest the data in a chart, the chart will work better on paper or on a personal-device screen, for someone who's not expected to listen to a presentation while trying to take in so much information. For example, health care policy makers might benefit from seeing this chart in advance of a hearing at which they'll discuss these long-term trends.

Our VP needs something cleaner for her context. She could make her point as simply as this:

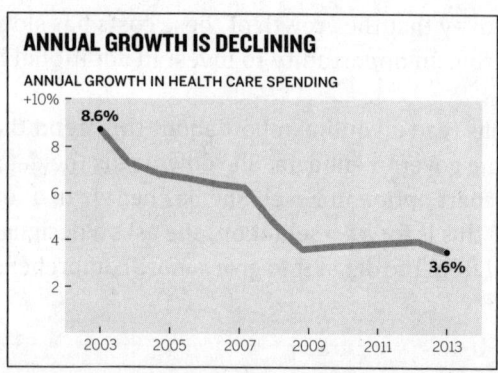

ANNUAL GROWTH IS DECLINING

ANNUAL GROWTH IN HEALTH CARE SPENDING

Simplicity like this takes some discipline—and courage—to achieve. The impulse is to include everything you know. Busy charts communicate the idea that you've been just that—busy. "Look at all the data I have and the work I've done," they seem to say. But that's not the VP's goal. She wants to persuade her colleagues to invest in new programs. With this chart, she won't have to utter a word for the executive team to understand the trend. She has clearly established a foundation for her recommendations.

In some ways, "data visualization" is a terrible term. It seems to reduce the construction of good charts to a mechanical procedure. It evokes the tools and methodology required to create rather than the creation itself. It's like calling *Moby-Dick* a "word sequentialization" or *The Starry Night* a "pigment distribution."

It also reflects an ongoing obsession in the dataviz world with process over outcomes. Visualization is merely a process. What we actually do when we make a good chart is get at some truth and move people to feel it—to see what couldn't be seen before. To change minds. To cause action.

Some basic common grammar will improve our ability to communicate visually. But good outcomes require a broader understanding and a strategic approach—which the typology described here is meant to help you develop.

Originally published in June 2016. Reprint R1606H

What Managers Need to Know About Social Tools

by Paul Leonardi and Tsedal Neeley

WORKPLACES HAVE ADOPTED internal social tools—think standalone technologies such as Slack, Yammer, and Chatter, or embedded applications such as Microsoft Teams and JIRA—at a staggering rate. In an ambitious study of 4,200 companies, conducted by the McKinsey Global Institute, 72% reported using them to facilitate employee communication. That figure grabbed our attention, so we asked leaders of both large and small organizations for more insight into why they were turning to social tools and platforms. They said things like "Other companies are, so we should too" and "That's what you have to do if you want to attract young talent." Although the bandwagon effect was not a surprise, this was: Few of the rationales were based on a solid business case, which leaders normally require when considering other technologies, such as CRM software or computer-simulation tools.

To more systematically identify the performance value that social tools can bring to companies, we split employees at a large financial services firm into two groups and observed them for six months. The first group used an internal social platform called Jive-n, while the other group did not.

The results were remarkable. The employees who had used the tool became 31% more likely to find coworkers with expertise relevant to meeting job goals. Those employees also became 88% more likely to accurately identify who could put them in contact with the right experts. They made these gains by observing what their coworkers talked about on Jive-n and with whom. The group that had no access to the tool showed no improvement on either measure over the same period.

Since then we have studied internal social tools in various work settings, including banking, insurance, telecommunications, e-commerce, atmospheric science, and computing. The mounting evidence is clear: These tools can promote employee collaboration and knowledge sharing across silos. They can help employees make faster decisions, develop more innovative ideas for products and services, and become more engaged in their work and their companies.

Over the past two decades organizations have sought some of these benefits through knowledge management databases, but with limited success. That's because determining who has expertise and understanding the context in which it was created are important parts of knowledge sharing. Databases do not provide that type of information and connection. Social tools do.

But we have found that companies that try to "go social," as many of them call it, often fall into four traps. Here we'll look at those traps and share recommendations for capitalizing on the promise of social tools.

Trap 1: Flawed Assumptions About Millennials

Leaders assume that young people "breathe" social media, as one senior executive at a large insurance company put it. This view of Millennials *outside* the workplace is certainly backed by good evidence—they're avid consumers of Facebook, Twitter, Instagram, Snapchat, Reddit, and countless dating sites. So managers often look to them to set an example in the organization, expecting that they will be pioneering users of social tools at work. But that's a mistake. In our extensive interviews and company surveys, we've found the opposite to be true. Millennials actually have a difficult time with

Idea in Brief

A Missed Opportunity

Internal social tools can improve collaboration, innovation, decision making, and employee engagement. But four common traps get in the way: Organizations make flawed assumptions about Millennials, struggle with personal and professional boundaries, overlook the learning that takes place, and derive faulty insights by focusing on the wrong data.

A Better Way

To realize the potential of social tools, organizations should clearly define why they're adopting them, encourage informal communication and even "lurking" to promote knowledge sharing and learning, and articulate the rules of conduct. And leaders should exhibit the behaviors they'd like to see from employees.

---

the notion that "social" tools can be used for "work" purposes, the way they might use a spreadsheet or a PowerPoint deck. They see social media as a space for self-expression and communication with friends and family. It's integral to their personal lives but—aside from LinkedIn and other career-building sites—it has little or nothing to do with their professional lives.

This may be in part because few Millennials encounter workplace technologies before college or their first serious jobs—at which point they have been active on social media for several years. They're wary of conflating those two worlds; they want to be viewed and treated as grown-ups now. "Friending" the boss is reminiscent of "friending" a parent back in high school—it's unsettling. And the word "social" signals "informal" and "personal." As a 23-year-old marketing analyst at a large telecommunications company told us, "You're on there to connect with your friends. It's weird to think that your manager would want you to connect with coworkers or that they'd want to connect with you on social media [at work]. I don't like that."

Most managers we have worked with want employees to use internal social tools to communicate informally about work—but not to discuss personal matters. Millennials aren't interested in crossing that line either, but they have trouble imagining how they *could* use social tools without getting personal.

Another problem is the way organizational leaders talk about the social tools they're implementing. In nearly every rollout we've seen, senior executives—trying to provide a cognitive link to a familiar technology—have referred to them as "Facebook for the company" or "Twitter for the company." But after hearing that from a manager, a 22-year-old data analyst at the insurance company mentioned above asked, "Why would I want to use Facebook at work? I don't think I necessarily want my boss knowing that I went to a party last night."

In our surveys, about 85% of young professionals said they struggle with social tools at work. Ironically, about 90% of older professionals viewed these tools as new and often useful modes of communication with their colleagues.

Trap 2: Repressing Informal Communication

The second trap is related to the first: Managers and other employees are generally not interested in sharing details about their *own* personal lives on social tools at work. Many companies even explicitly prohibit the discussion of nonwork topics on their internal sites. And yet we find that a key motivator for employees to engage with their company's social tools is curiosity about *others'* personal lives. That's true for people of all ages and ranks.

Although such voyeurism might seem problematic at first glance, our research shows that it's a missed opportunity, because it can make work interactions easier and more productive. It's hard to strike up a conversation with someone you don't know well. It's even more difficult to ask that person for help or a favor. Employees feel better equipped for such exchanges when they have gained personal insights about their coworkers by watching them communicate on internal social tools. Our research at a large telecommunications company, for example, revealed that employees who do so are three times as likely as others to get pertinent *work* information from colleagues.

Jose, a mid-level manager in the telecom company's marketing division, shared an illustrative story about connecting with his coworker Alex: "I was following [on the company's Chatter site] this guy in the e-commerce division who posted about soccer statistics. I thought it was cool and interesting because it was a hobby of mine too. So I went to his page to see if he'd written anything about the Euro Cup, and I saw a communication between him and another guy in marketing about a promotion they were working on. I was like, 'Whoa, this promotion is a great idea.' So I called him up and introduced myself and told him I kind of stalked him because of his soccer posts, and we both laughed. And then I said, 'Hey, I saw [your posts] about this promotion you're doing. Can you tell me about it so we maybe could do something like this in my division?'" Like many other employees we talked to, Jose was drawn to a particular coworker because of a shared interest. That gave him material for his opening bid for important work-related knowledge.

By watching colleagues talk about hobbies and pastimes on internal social tools, employees can also assess whether their coworkers are likable. An engineer at a large e-commerce company told us that he often did this to "size people up" and determine how "safe" they were to approach. Others made similar comments. How coworkers responded to people's queries or joked around suggested how accessible they were; it helped colleagues gauge what we call "passable trust" (whether somebody is trustworthy enough to share information with). That's important, because asking people to help solve a problem is an implicit admission that you can't do it alone. It can make you feel vulnerable, especially if you're afraid of developing a reputation for lacking certain knowledge.

Still, as valuable as it may be to observe personal, informal communication at work, our investigation kept bringing us back to this paradox: The content that attracts people to their companies' social tools and keeps them coming back can also inhibit them. Employees often worry that interaction on these tools will be seen as wasting time—and many managers do assume that productivity is suffering when they see a lot of chitchat there. If internal social tools are to deliver on their promise, companies and individuals must become comfortable with both personal and professional interactions online.

Trap 3: Failure to Recognize Learning

Lew Platt, a former CEO of Hewlett-Packard, was fond of saying, "If only HP knew what HP knows, we would be three times more productive." Our work shows that internal social tools provide a space for employees to acquire knowledge by watching their colleagues. But when we asked more than 400 people across various companies to tell us what they had learned on these tools, we got blank stares. The most common response was "Nothing." That's because learning on social tools happens at a remove, while others go about their work, so people don't think of it as learning.

It's actually a bit like spying or eavesdropping. Research shows that people spend much more time as "lurkers" or "observers" on social tools than they do as content producers—writing posts, sharing information, or creating documents and videos. We've found that people can acquire at least two types of knowledge this way: *direct knowledge* and *metaknowledge.*

Employees gather direct knowledge when they observe others' communications about solving problems. Take Reagan, an IT technician at a large atmospheric research lab. She happened to see on her department's social site that a colleague, Jamie, had sent a message to another technician, Brett, about how to fix a semantic key encryption issue. Reagan said, "I'm so happy I saw that message. Jamie explained it so well that I was able to learn how to do it." Employees share this kind of information with one another all the time in hallway conversations and e-mails. But because Jamie and Brett decided to communicate via the company's social site, their exchange was visible to Reagan, too, and she learned something unexpected and useful.

Employees who gain metaknowledge don't learn how to *do* something; instead they learn who has the expertise they need or who knows someone who has it. Consider Amanda, a marketing coordinator at the financial services firm mentioned above. Her manager asked her to analyze trends in an enormous data set, and she was unsure how best to structure the report query. After trying (unsuccessfully) to figure it out by herself, she decided to log on to the company's internal social tool to see if anyone had posted documentation that would help her. She couldn't find any, but she did see an exchange between two employees in marketing—Rick and Alicia—who were discussing that very issue. Rick recommended that Alicia contact Mark, in the analytics department, because he knew how to write the proper script.

Excited, Amanda left Mark a voicemail asking for help. She didn't get a response, so she tried again the next day—still no response. Fortunately, by observing the conversation between Rick and Alicia, she had learned not only "who knows what" but also "who knows whom"—both important components of metaknowledge. So she asked Rick if he would broker an introduction. Rick texted Mark to ask if Amanda could talk with him about writing a script, and Mark texted back immediately to say that she could call him in five minutes. Amanda called, Mark wrote the script, and Amanda estimates that she saved nearly a week's worth of time on her project.

Employees who observe others' communications pick up bits and pieces of seemingly unimportant information over time. Eventually they begin to form a picture of who knows what and whom. As the tech writer Clive Thompson has observed, using social tools is like staring at a pointillist painting. No dot by itself makes much sense. But when you step back to see all the dots together, you comprehend a rich image. The slow process whereby people see the individual dots makes it difficult for them to realize they are learning. Unless managers explicitly highlight the potential for knowledge sharing and skill building when rolling out social tools—and have developmental conversations with employees—people may underutilize or even abandon them.

Trap 4: Focusing on the Wrong Data

Employees' communications and behaviors become highly visible on internal social tools, which can make it easier to collaborate. But not all that is visible is important or useful. Sometimes social content leads people to focus—and act—on the wrong data.

To illustrate, let's return to the atmospheric research lab. A reorganization brought together IT technicians who had never collaborated before. At first they relied on seniority as a proxy for expertise—they sought advice from their most seasoned colleagues. To help them share knowledge more effectively and learn who knew what and whom, the IT director implemented a social tool for the department. As is usually the case, employees started using it slowly. But as communication on the site increased, people began to read messages between coworkers about solutions they had devised for computing and network problems across the lab. Eventually it became clear that Jill, the most junior technician in the department, was actually the most knowledgeable in certain areas—and people started turning to her with questions.

Peggy, the group's most senior technician, quit after several months of this, frustrated that her coworkers, who had initially come to her for help and advice, no longer seemed interested in her recommendations. Her colleagues were very clear about why they had shifted from Peggy to Jill: Jill's messages and posts were chock-full of useful technical details. One coworker noted, "Jill just seems to really know a lot about the issues I face."

The IT director was not sad to see Peggy leave. He reasoned that the social tool had exposed the fact that she was not as knowledgeable as everyone had thought, and he was pleased that his employees were now going to the "smartest" person for help. But barely two months after Peggy's departure, the IT department's evaluations from scientists across the organization plummeted. Peggy might not have been the most technically sophisticated employee in the department, but she had the most cultural and political knowledge. She knew which scientists' problems should be highest priority, and she knew what preferences various scientists had for technology in their labs.

Because the technicians were thinking of "expertise" solely as technical knowledge, Peggy's value to the group was hidden. To salvage the department's customer satisfaction scores, the IT manager hired Peggy back at a 30% premium and began to encourage her and others in the department to diversify the types of knowledge they shared on the site.

Across all the companies we studied, the most visible information and knowledge were perceived as most important. If employees' contributions and strengths weren't showing up in their posts or messages, they were likely to be overlooked—and the organization wouldn't benefit from them. Our findings support the old adage that what gets recorded gets remembered.

Capitalizing on Social Tools at Work

Although these four traps are common, your organization needn't fall into them. In our consulting work we've found that to reap the benefits of internal social tools, companies can define the purpose, strengthen ambient awareness, spell out rules of conduct, and lead by example.

Define the purpose.

Most employees don't know exactly why they're meant to use internal social tools. As a result, people may shy away from them—or, without realizing it, use them in ways that undermine rather than enhance performance. For instance, at the financial services company in which we did our experiment, executives hadn't made it clear that one of their goals was to strengthen employee relationships. Consequently, many employees grew afraid over time that management—after observing what they shared online—would think they were "socializing" too much at work. So they began to disengage from the site, even though they thought it provided value. It takes a critical mass of employees to make internal social tools useful. Thus leaders need to clearly explain what employees and the organization as a whole stand to gain through these new technologies. We have found the following to be the most significant ways social tools provide value in organizations:

Improving collaboration. Internal social tools can enable employees to engage with coworkers more widely, building awareness of expertise and increasing collaboration across the organization. That's what happened when Jose, the manager at the telecom company, parlayed his coworker Alex's love of soccer into a productive partnership. Their initial conversation sparked other discussions about common issues in their respective departments. They hatched an idea to develop a new branding campaign (using Jose's marketing expertise) for one of Alex's businesses (in the e-commerce division) that ended up increasing customer retention by more than 200%. Alex said, "No one from my department had ever worked with marketing before. Who knew we could complement each other so well?"

Enhancing knowledge sharing. Companies are increasingly using social tools to gain a competitive advantage through internal knowledge sharing. Often this benefit emerges organically and is then put to strategic use. For example, a group of engineers at a large e-commerce company struck up a useful conversation on Yammer. One engineer in the German office learned about a web-analytics application that the more advanced Tokyo office had implemented locally. He contacted a Tokyo engineer to get detailed information about the application and the network environment required to support it and then adopted the application and posted his satisfaction with it to the group. American and French engineers expressed interest in the tool for their local markets. Observing its success in Tokyo and Germany and its potential elsewhere, the manager of the group required that it be adopted across all markets. We observed a similar spread of knowledge in the marketing, sales, and legal groups.

Creating a connected global company. Employees who work in different locations around the world often have a hard time building relationships and forging a shared identity. Social tools can facilitate personal and professional connections, increasing trust and rapport across geographic and cultural borders. Many global employees report that internal social tools give them a window onto broader organizational discourse that is otherwise unavailable to them. As Sam, who works for the e-commerce company, explained, "I get a feel for what everyone's doing over there [at headquarters], the types of projects, and how they're doing. So I definitely feel more connected."

Others at the company echoed Sam's sentiment, saying, "I feel like I am part of the family" and "We're the same company. We're the same people. We look different, we might sound different, but we're doing the same thing at the end of the day." In a dynamic and global marketplace, far-flung employees value this sense of belonging.

Preventing duplication of work. Social tools allow employees to learn about existing projects and initiatives that overlap with their own and to coordinate efforts. This can reduce work duplication and free up time and money to generate new knowledge. At the insurance company we studied, one employee, Sheila, was asked by her manager to put a hold on her current project and perform an urgent analysis for a new vertical market. She told her manager that the analysis would most likely take two weeks, pushing her current project past the deadline and over budget. The manager was willing to pay that price. As Sheila began to dig into the problem, she remembered a series of exchanges on the internal social tool among colleagues in another department about a project they were working on in that same vertical market. With this metaknowledge, she sent them a note asking if they could suggest where to start. They replied that they had completed a market analysis and asked if she would like to see it. Sheila said that when she received the report, "I couldn't believe it. It was exactly what my boss asked me to do. This just saved me two weeks, and it saved my project over a million dollars. I had no idea they were working on this. Neither did my boss."

Increasing innovation. With the help of social tools, employees can sometimes borrow ideas and solutions from other parts of the organization and combine them in fresh ways to create new products or processes. A clear example of innovation comes from the financial services firm we studied. Tim, an employee in the consumer finance division, was working out the details of a new loan program. He couldn't quite figure out how to make his idea work. But then inspiration struck: "I suddenly remembered that I'd seen a communication exchanged between these two guys. . . . One of them, Joe

Franklin, who's in the pricing department, mentioned something—I forget the context—about rate variation depending upon risk factors. That caught my eye, so I read the history of the conversation he had, and it turns out that there was some flexibility in rate assignment based on risk class. I sent him an e-mail to see if I could learn more about it, and it made sense. So I developed the program around it, and it's been pretty successful so far—really innovative, so it made me proud."

Tim's director was very happy too. The product came in on time and under budget, and carved out a new niche for the company in a crowded market.

Social tools bring the greatest benefits when employees are exposed to ideas and insights from people across the organization—particularly people they wouldn't normally encounter. The challenge, however, is that focusing attention on content coming from multiple departments—many of which have different goals and may seem unrelated to one's own work—is difficult. For this reason, organizations tend to deploy social tools within departments. But if patterns of communication are too insular, the expanded network that these tools promise won't materialize.

Once you've defined your organization's key purpose and made a plan for deploying social tools, clearly articulate all that through internal marketing campaigns, messaging from the top, and one-on-one or group training sessions to focus employees' efforts.

Strengthen ambient awareness.

Whatever purpose you define, you'll be more likely to achieve it if you allow the tools to hone employees' "ambient awareness"—a social-science term for awareness of communication and behavior around you in which you are not directly involved. You can do this in a couple of ways. First, make clear to everyone that management sees the value of friendly interaction—even when it has nothing to do with work. And then let it happen. That's how people make unexpected fruitful connections across the organization. If you see some chattiness online and start to worry about lost productivity, quash the urge to limit exchanges to "work only" topics. Encourage people to befriend and follow new coworkers—preferably in other departments or divisions—instead of solely paying attention to those they already talk to off-line. They'll develop a richer sense of who knows what and whom. Second, occasionally remind employees that it's productive to absorb seemingly unimportant or uninteresting details about their colleagues. Noticing that someone is working on closing a deal with a wireless antenna company may not seem immediately relevant to an employee. But it's still important to file that sort of detail away—it may become useful later. And every piece of information contributes to a full, vibrant picture of the organization.

Spell out rules of conduct.

Companies often have three concerns about employee behavior on internal social tools: that it is too informal, that people can share confidential information, and that people might inadvertently violate externally mandated regulatory policies. The first concern is misplaced. The emerging norm is casual, brief communication, and for good reason: Though formality may be appropriate for other channels (such as e-mails to superiors or memos to the staff), it thwarts the kind of information exchange and knowledge flow you want to see on social tools.

However, it's critical to address the other two concerns—respecting confidentiality and adhering to regulations. This involves managing visibility. Not all social communications should be made public. Leaders must be clear about which types of information and data cannot be shared broadly—client account numbers and revenue projections, for instance—and which can.

Lead by example.

Finally, people take their behavioral cues from above. If leaders aren't present on internal social tools, employees won't be either. And if leaders post mostly formal announcements about changes in policy or personnel (which happens often), employees will view the tools as just another vehicle for management to broadcast information, rather than as a way for them to communicate with one another. The organization will fail to achieve its purpose for implementing social tools.

As with any initiative that requires cultural change, leaders must model the behavior they would like to see. When they notice a good idea streaming on their company's social tool, they should publicly engage the person who posted it. And when employees share information that's not related to work, leaders should chime in with interest.

Bringing social tools into a company may look simple. Most of them are cloud-based applications, so they require virtually no investment in infrastructure. What's more, today's employees have experience using social media in their personal lives, making the learning curve easy for most people. But belying this apparent simplicity is a much more complicated reality: To achieve the benefits of a social enterprise, companies must work hard to avoid the common traps we've described—traps that can ensnare even the most adventurous enterprise. Some of the organizations we've studied have succeeded by using the strategies in this article. As a result, their employees are more engaged with their global companies, do a better job of communicating and sharing skills and knowledge, and collaborate and innovate more effectively.

Originally published in November–December 2017. R1706J

Be Yourself, But Carefully

by Lisa Rosh and Lynn Offermann

"AUTHENTICITY" IS THE NEW BUZZWORD among leaders today. We're told to bring our full selves to the office, to engage in frank conversations, and to tell personal stories as a way of gaining our colleagues' trust and improving group performance. The rise in collaborative workplaces and dynamic teams over recent years has only heightened the demand for "instant intimacy," and managers are supposed to set an example.

But the honest sharing of thoughts, feelings, and experiences at work is a double-edged sword: Despite its potential benefits, self-disclosure can backfire if it's hastily conceived, poorly timed, or inconsistent with cultural or organizational norms—hurting your reputation, alienating employees, fostering distrust, and hindering teamwork. Getting it right takes a deft touch, for leaders at any stage of their careers.

Consider Mitch, the director of a newly established department at a major U.S. university, who was responsible for negotiating and maintaining links with other educational and research institutions. Attempting to break the ice in his first meeting with the dean of a prominent college, he mentioned how excited he was to be at the dean's school, because he'd wanted to attend it but had been rejected. He got a cold stare in response, and the meeting ended without an agreement. Mitch thought his comment was friendly and self-deprecating; now he realizes that it probably lowered his standing with the dean, who may have thought he was either challenging the admissions process or seeking pity. Mitch learned that such revelations must be skillfully deployed.

In our years of studying and consulting on leadership development, team building, and communication skills, we've come across hundreds of cases like this. Drawing on them and on more than four decades' worth of research in social and organizational psychology, we now have some lessons to share. Here we look at the common mistakes executives make when they're trying to be authentic and offer a five-step plan for moving toward more-effective self-disclosure.

Where Leaders Slip

Authenticity begins with self-awareness: knowing who you are—your values, emotions, and competencies—and how you're perceived by others. Only then can you know what to reveal and when. Good communication skills are also key to effective self-disclosure; your stories are worthwhile only if you can express them well. We typically encounter three types of executives whose lack of self-knowledge causes their revelations to fall flat—oblivious leaders, bumblers, and open books—and two types who fail because they are poor communicators: inscrutable leaders and social engineers. (However, people often fit into more than one category at least some of the time.)

Oblivious leaders don't have a realistic view of themselves and thus reveal information and opinions in a manner that appears clueless or phony. Take Lori, the director of sales and business development for a global software company. She sees herself as an inclusive, participatory, and team-oriented manager and likes to tell stories about her time as a junior staff member and how much she valued having a voice in decisions. But her subordinates consider her to be highly directive and thus find her anecdotes disingenuous. As one employee puts it, "I don't care if you make every decision, but don't pretend to care about my opinion."

Idea in Brief

A rise in collaborative workplaces and dynamic teams over recent years has heightened the demand for "authenticity" and "instant intimacy," and managers are supposed to set an example. But sharing thoughts, feelings, and experiences at work can backfire if it's hastily conceived, poorly timed, or inconsistent with cultural or organizational norms.

To avoid common mistakes, leaders should follow a five-step plan for moving toward more effective self-disclosure.

1. **Build a foundation of self-knowledge.** Solicit honest feedback from coworkers and follow it up with coaching.

2. **Consider relevance to the task.** Before sharing personal information, ask yourself if it's germane to the situation.

3. **Keep revelations genuine.** Making up or exaggerating stories is easily discovered and can damage credibility.

4. **Understand the organizational and cultural context.** Some societies are more inclined than others to disclose personal information.

5. **Delay or avoid very personal disclosures.** First take note of how open others are.

The authors include a tool to help you assess when—and when not—to share.

Bumblers have a better understanding of who they are but not of how they come across to others. Unable to read colleagues' social cues, including body language and facial expressions, they make ill-timed, inappropriate disclosures or opt out of relationship building altogether. This behavior is particularly prevalent in cross-cultural situations when people aren't attuned to differing social norms. A case in point involves Roger, a partner in a multinational consulting firm who was assigned to help boost market share for the firm's newly formed Asia-Pacific office. Asked to coach a team that had recently lost an important account, he decided to share a story about losing his first client. In the United States, anecdotes about his own mistakes had always made his subordinates feel better. But Roger's Asian colleagues were dismayed that their new leader would risk his honor, reputation, and influence by admitting weakness.

You don't need to leave your country to bumble. Take Anne, the general manager of a cafeteria for an international technology company. An extrovert who knows herself well, she shares her experiences and perceptions freely. This can be effective when she's talking to her staff, but it's less so with outsiders. For example, when an HR manager recently complimented her on the catering she'd coordinated for an in-house awards ceremony, Anne thanked him and went on to disclose that she'd been concerned because the company had come close to outsourcing its food service. Instead of seizing an opportunity to secure more internal business for her beleaguered cafeteria, she diminished her status and worried team members who overheard the exchange.

Open books talk endlessly about themselves, about others, about everything; they're too comfortable communicating. So although colleagues may seek them out as sources of information, they ultimately don't trust them. Consider Jeremy, an outgoing senior manager with a sharp mind but a string of failed management consulting engagements. When people first meet him, his warmth, intelligence, and ability to draw them into conversation make them feel as if he were an old friend. But his aggressive familiarity soon wears thin ("I know more about his wife than I know about my own," one former colleague says), and his bosses question whether he's discreet enough for client work. Indeed, Jeremy was asked to leave his most recent job after he used a key meeting with a prospective client to detail work he'd done for several others, not only outlining their problems but identifying them by name.

Inscrutable leaders are at the other end of the spectrum: They have difficulty sharing anything about themselves in the workplace, so they come off as remote and inaccessible and can't create long-term office relationships. Aviva is a registered dietician who expanded her private practice into a full-service nutritional guidance, exercise training, and health products company. Although she's talented and passionate, she has difficulty retaining employees, because she fails to communicate her enthusiasm and long-term vision. Recently featured on a panel of female entrepreneurs, she opted to present a basic annual report and outline her sales strategy rather than to captivate the audience with a personal story, as others had done. Afterward, the other panelists were flooded with résumés and business cards; Aviva had lost out on the significant benefits that can come from appropriate self-revelation.

Finally, *social engineers* are similar to inscrutable leaders in that they don't instinctively share, and to bumblers in that they often have difficulty reading social cues, but their chief shortcoming is the way they encourage self-disclosure within their work groups. Instead of modeling desired behaviors, they sponsor external activities such as off-site team building. Andrew, for example, is a unit head at a financial services firm with an ultracompetitive corporate culture. Every year, he sends his team on a mandatory retreat run by an outside consultant who demands personal revelations in artificial settings. Yet Andrew never models or encourages self-disclosure in the office—and he looks the other way if employees exploit colleagues' self-revealed weaknesses to get ahead. When we asked one of Andrew's direct reports about the most recent group getaway, she said, "I learned that I hate my colleagues—and my manager—even more than I thought."

Executives who make any or all of these mistakes may appear to be simply incompetent. But their cautionary tales are much more common than you might think, and we can all learn from them. In our work we've seen even the most self-aware, talented communicators err in how, when, or to whom they reveal a personal story. Everyone should understand best practices in self-disclosure.

A Five-Step Path

Let's return to Mitch, who blundered with the college dean. Chastened by that experience, he vowed to get better at revelation. Since then his disclosures have proved far more effective, allowing him to establish many enduring partnerships. What makes him so successful now? First, he's self-aware: He knows who he is, where he came from, where he's going, and what he believes in. He encourages colleagues to give him feedback, and he's enrolled in several developmental training programs. Second, he communicates cautiously, letting the task at hand, along with environmental cues, dictate what to reveal when. For instance, he was all business at one meeting with a potential partner until she voiced a concern about whether her students could assimilate at his university. Sensing a critical moment in the negotiation, he decided to tell her about the challenges he'd faced in an exchange program during college—trying to learn another language, make friends, and adjust to the curriculum. The story was personal and heartfelt but also demonstrated an understanding of his counterpart's concern and a commitment to addressing it. He deepened the relationship and sealed the deal.

Mitch arrived at effective, authentic self-disclosure by following five steps:

1. Build a foundation of self-knowledge.

You can learn about yourself in many ways, but the best approach is to solicit honest feedback—ideally a 360-degree review—from coworkers and follow it up with coaching. In *Why Should Anyone Be Led by You?* (Harvard Business School Press, 2006), Rob Goffee and Gareth Jones suggest exploring biography. You might consider your upbringing, your work experiences, and new situations, such as volunteer opportunities, that test your comfort zone and force you to reflect on your values. You might also consider your personal management philosophy and the events and people who shaped it. We start our executive coaching engagements with a detailed interview that essentially walks clients through their personal and professional histories, their successes and failures, and the lessons they've drawn as a result. These exercises can help you choose which stories are most appropriate to share with others.

2. Consider relevance to the task.

Skillful self-disclosers choose the substance, process, and timing of revelations to further the task at hand, not to promote themselves or create purely personal relationships. In fact, we found in our earlier work that team development efforts often fail because they try too hard to foster intimacy rather than focusing on task-relevant disclosure and social cohesion. Be clear that your goal in revealing yourself at work is to build trust and engender better collaboration and team-work, not to make friends—though that may happen. So before you share personal information, ask yourself whether it will help you do your job. Is it germane to the situation? Will your staff get a better understanding of your thinking and rationale? If not, you might want to save the story for a coffee date with friends. If your goal is simply to develop rapport with employees, you can find safer ways to accomplish that—such as bonding over a beloved sports team, a new movie, or a favorite restaurant.

3. Keep revelations genuine.

This should be a no-brainer, but we're amazed at how often we hear about managers who fabricate tales. Take Allan, who recently stepped down from his position as the associate director of marketing and communications for a regional hotel chain. In both presentations and small group discussions, he would cite examples of how he had successfully used social media, video on demand, and search engine optimization in his prior position at a premier boutique hotel. The problem was that he held that job in the early 1980s, before those technologies were widespread. Allan did have extensive social media marketing experience, but it had come through his volunteer church work; he fudged the details in an effort to bond with his younger colleagues. Eventually they found out, and Allan lost credibility, which ultimately led to his departure from the company. Making up stories or exaggerating parts of a narrative to fit the situation may seem like a good idea, but it is easily discovered and can do a lot of harm. Instead try to find real if less-than-perfect disclosures that still capture the emotions of the situation and convey empathy. If, for example, Mitch had never been part of an exchange program, he might have told his potential partner that he was a father and therefore recognized the importance of assuaging young people's fears in new situations.

4. Understand the organizational and cultural context.

Considerable research has shown that people from individualistic societies, such as the United States and India, are more likely

When—and When Not—to Share

THIS CHECKLIST CAN HELP you decide when self-disclosure is advisable.

How much self-reflection have you done?

A. I don't engage in self-reflection.

B. I've taken many self-assessment tests but rarely get feedback from others.

C. I've completed numerous self-assessments, and my scores are usually similar to those my colleagues give me in 360-degree reviews.

What is your goal in self-disclosure?

A. I want to demonstrate knowledge, competence, or empathy.

B. I want to connect with my colleagues in order to improve the atmosphere at work.

C. I want to gain the trust of my colleagues in order to make our performance more effective.

What kinds of information do you disclose?

A. I fabricate a story to fit the situation.

B. I tell a true story that may or may not fit the situation.

---

to disclose information about themselves and expect others to do the same than people from collectivist societies, such as China and Japan. Thus Roger's Asian teammates might have been put off by his readiness to share a personal story, regardless of its content. Make an effort to investigate national and organizational norms about sharing so that you'll know when it's best to keep quiet. In any context, but especially one new to you that involves teammates from other countries, companies, or functions, you should talk to respected insiders about how people operate and what level of candor is expected. HR personnel and group leaders may be able to provide this information, but you can also test the waters with taskrelevant self-disclosure to see how people respond. And you can look for cues such as eye contact and others' attempts to share or solicit stories.

    C. I tell a true story that fits the emotion of the situation and conveys empathy.

What personal information do your colleagues share with you?

    A. No one shares personal information in my workplace.

    B. I know a lot about the personal lives of a few friends at work but not much about my other colleagues.

    C. My colleagues share personal information, especially when it is pertinent to the task.

How long have you known your colleagues?

    A. We just met.

    B. We've had one or two formal meetings.

    C. We've had at least a week of formal and informal discussions and have completed one significant task.

If your answers were mostly As, you might want to be quiet.

If they were mostly Bs, you should proceed cautiously.

If they were mostly Cs, speak up.

5. Delay or avoid very personal disclosures.

Intimate stories *strengthen* relationships; they don't establish them. Sharing too much personal information too quickly breaks all sociocultural norms of behavior, making one appear awkward, needy, or even unstable. That was Helen's mistake when she was asked to introduce herself at the cross-site launch of a training program at her home health care agency. Exhausted after a sleepless night with her sick baby, she shared that experience in her introduction, to the discomfort of her audience. "They wanted to know about my education and industry background, and instead I spoke graphically about baby throw-up," she recalls. "It took me a few months after that to reestablish credibility." This doesn't mean you have to wait years before telling colleagues anything about your personal life. You just need to have spent enough time with them to develop a foundation of trust and to learn organizational norms. First develop common objectives, delineate goals and roles, and demonstrate credibility and trustworthiness through your work. Take careful note of how open others are before offering significant disclosures of your own. In some workplaces you will eventually find it safe and helpful to share; in others you'll realize it's extremely unwise to do so.

These five steps should help you avoid some of the pitfalls we've outlined and become a more effective leader. Remember to think carefully about your motives and likelihood of success. (See the sidebar "When—and When Not—to Share.") Self-disclosure is a valuable managerial tool, but it must be used judiciously. What stories do you have to tell, and who needs to hear them?

Originally published in October 2013. Reprint R1310J

How to Preempt Team Conflict

by Ginka Toegel and Jean-Louis Barsoux

TEAM CONFLICT CAN ADD VALUE OR DESTROY IT. Good conflict fosters respectful debate and yields mutually agreed-upon solutions that are often far superior to those first offered. Bad conflict occurs when team members simply can't get past their differences, killing productivity and stifling innovation.

Disparate opinions aren't the root of the problem, however. Most destructive conflict stems from something deeper: a perceived incompatibility in the way various team members operate due to any number of factors, including personality, industry, race, gender, and age. The conventional approach to working through such conflict is to respond to clashes as they arise or wait until there is clear evidence of a problem before addressing it. But these approaches routinely fail because they allow frustrations to build for too long, making it difficult to reset negative impressions and restore trust.

In our 25 years of researching team dynamics, coaching teams in *Fortune* 500 corporations, and teaching thousands of executives at Duke University, London Business School, and IMD, we've found that a proactive approach is much more effective. When you surface differences before a team starts work—even when the group seems homogeneous and harmonious—you can preempt destructive conflict.

We have developed and tested a methodology that focuses on five areas: how people look, act, speak, think, and feel. Team leaders facilitate a series of 20- to 30-minute conversations, encouraging members to express their preferences and expectations in each area, identify the most likely areas of misalignment or friction, and come up with suggestions for how those with differing expectations can work together. Through the nonjudgmental exchange of ideas and feedback, teams establish a foundation of trust and understanding and are able to set ground rules for effective collaboration.

Though setting aside time for these conversations up front might seem onerous, we've found that it's a worthwhile investment for any team—new or old, C-suite or frontline—that will be collaborating on significant work for an extended period of time. Leaders need no special training to facilitate the discussions. Indeed, we've found that managers can master these conflict-prevention skills far more easily than those required for conflict resolution.

Five Conversations

Because the five conversations we propose go so far beyond typical "getting to know you" chitchat, it's important to kick them off properly. First, although this may seem obvious, make sure to include everyone on the team and explain why you're initiating the discussions. You might say something like: "Working on a team means collaborating with people whose approaches may differ from your own. Let's explore these differences now, while the pressure is off, so that they don't catch us by surprise and generate unproductive conflict at an inopportune moment." Explain that the focus of the discussions will be on the *process* of work rather than the *content*.

As the facilitator, make sure that people are comfortable sharing at their own pace and coach them on how to ask clarifying, nonjudgmental questions of one another. Encourage everyone to begin statements with "In my world . . ." and questions with "In your world . . .?" This phrasing, borrowed from organizational behavior scholar Edgar Schein, reinforces the idea that underlying sources of differences are irrelevant. What does matter is the attitudes and behaviors expressed as a result of each person's cumulative personal

Idea in Brief

The Problem

Team conflict erupts not because of differences in opinion but because of a perceived incompatibility in the way different team members think and act. When people can't get past their differences, the resulting clashes kill productivity and stifle innovation.

An Alternative View

Differences in perspective and experience can generate great value, of course. A new methodology helps leaders guide their teams through five conversations before work starts, to build shared understanding and lay the foundation for effective collaboration.

In Practice

The approach focuses on the *process* of work rather than the *content*. Leaders facilitate targeted discussions that explore the varying ways team members look, act, speak, think, and feel, to immunize the team against unproductive conflict when the pressure is on.

and professional experience. For example, the fact that you are assertive may be related to your personality, gender, or culture, but the only thing your colleagues need to know is that you tend to vocalize your opinions in plain terms.

Team members are likely to be hesitant as you begin, so ease everyone into the process by volunteering to share first. Once the dialogue gains steam, let others guide (but not dominate) it. Eventually, people will move from superficial disclosures to deeper discussion. As they listen to the responses of others and offer their own, they will develop not only a better understanding of their colleagues but also greater self-awareness.

The five topics can be addressed in any order; however, we've found the sequence presented here to be the most logical, especially with new teams, because we perceive first how others look and then how they speak and act. Only after observing them for a longer period can we infer how they think or feel. That said, facilitators should not get hung up on the categories, because there is inevitable overlap. Likewise, if participants struggle with the "In my world" language, it can be tweaked.

Let's now consider the five categories in turn.

Look: Questions to Ask

In your world:

- What makes a good first impression? A bad one?
- What do you notice first about others (dress, speech, demeanor)?
- What does that make you think about them (rigid, pushy, lazy)?
- What intangible credentials do you value (education, experience, connections)?
- How do you perceive status difference?

Look: Spotting the Difference

Colleagues routinely make fast judgments (especially negative ones) about the character, competence, or status of their peers on the basis of the briefest exposure—what Nalini Ambady and Robert Rosenthal, in research conducted at Harvard, called "thin slices" of behavior. These reactions are often triggered by differences in the way people present themselves. We unconsciously respond to cues in how they look, move, and dress, in their tone of voice, and in what they say about themselves.

The goal of this conversation is to help team members reflect on how they intend to come across to others—and how they actually do. A good place to begin is a discussion about the drivers of status in team members' respective "worlds." For example, some people put a premium on job-related characteristics, such as experience, connections, and functional background. For others, status is linked to demographic cues such as age, gender, nationality, and education. Team members can quickly put colleagues off by emphasizing the wrong credentials, adopting an unsuitable persona, or even dressing inappropriately for the culture. One executive from the "buttoned-up" banking sector faced this type of conflict when he joined an advertising group. In a team discussion, one of his colleagues told him, "The norm here is business casual. So by wearing a suit and tie at all times, it's like you think you're special, and that creates distance."

A similar situation arose at a heavy-engineering company when a female designer joined its board. Her colorful clothing and introductory comments, which included two literary references, made her pragmatic peers think she valued style over substance, which set her up to be marginalized.

An example that highlights the value of discussing perceptions up front comes from a global food group, where a leadership-development rotation of promising young executives had been creating resentment among older subsidiary executives, most notably in the Australian operation. The local team had developed a dysfunctional "keep your head down" attitude and simply tolerated each ambitious MBA until he or she moved on. But when one incoming manager engaged his team in the five conversations at the start of his term, he was able to dispel their negative preconceptions and develop far-more-productive relationships than his predecessors had.

Act: Misjudging Behavior

On diverse teams, clashing behavioral norms are common sources of trouble. Seemingly trivial gestures can have a disproportionate impact, aggravating stereotypes, alienating people, and disrupting communication flows.

Physical boundaries are often a problem area. Consider the media firestorm that retired French soccer player Thierry Henry set off when, as a TV pundit reacting to surprising breaking news, he touched the thigh of his male English colleague. French culture accepts that sort of interaction, but for television studio colleagues in the macho world of British football, it was a step too far. Or consider the introverted, high-anxiety executive we worked with whose warm and gregarious peer made him uncomfortable: Their expectations for the proper distance at which to interact differed starkly. "I was taking a coffee with him at one of those standing tables," he remembers. "We literally shuffled round the table as he moved toward me and I tried to reestablish my buffer zone."

Act: Questions to Ask

In your world:

- How important are punctuality and time limits?
- Are there consequences of being late or missing deadlines?
- What is a comfortable physical distance for interacting in the workplace?
- Should people volunteer for assignments or wait to be nominated?
- What group behaviors are valued (helping others, not complaining)?

Attitudes about time can stir up conflict, too. People differ widely—even within the same firm or department—with regard to the importance of being punctual and respectful of other people's schedules. More broadly, the value of keeping projects on pace and hitting milestone deadlines may be paramount to some, whereas others may value flexibility and the ability to nimbly respond as circumstances unfold. An example comes from a Nordic industrial machinery company that had recurrent tensions in the top team. The non-Nordic executives in the group were deeply frustrated by what they saw as a lack of urgency shown by their Nordic colleagues, and they responded with brusqueness—which, of course, upset their peers. Eventually, the group discussed the situation and set new rules of engagement. But a preemptive conversation would have saved them all a great deal of time and energy.

Differing levels of assertiveness between team members can present problems as well. Male executives, for example, or people from individualistic corporate and national cultures, often feel quite comfortable volunteering for special assignments or nominating themselves to take on additional responsibilities because they consider it a sign of commitment, competence, and self-confidence. But others may see those actions as blatant, undignified, and shallow self-promotion. Expectations for how much colleagues should help one another, as opposed to contributing individually to the group effort, can also vary widely. For example, a team of software engineers ran into problems when it became clear that some members were very selective in giving aid to peers, while others did so whenever asked.

Speak: Questions to Ask

In your world:

- Is a promise an aspiration or a guarantee?
- Which is most important: directness or harmony?
- Are irony and sarcasm appreciated?
- Do interruptions signal interest or rudeness?
- Does silence mean reflection or disengagement?
- Should dissenting views be aired in public or discussed off-line?
- Is unsolicited feedback welcome?

Those who spent more time helping others understandably began to feel resentful and disadvantaged, since doing so often interfered with their own work. It's important to establish team norms around all these behaviors up front to avoid unnecessary antagonism.

Speak: Dividing by Language

Communication styles have many dimensions—the words people choose to express themselves, tolerance for candor, humor, pauses and interruptions, and so on—and the possibilities for misunderstanding are endless.

Teams made up of people with different native languages present significant challenges in this area. But even when everyone is fluent in a particular language, there may be deep differences in how individuals express themselves. For example, depending on context, culture, and other factors, "yes" can mean "maybe" or "let's try it" or even "no way." At a European software firm we worked with, two executives were at each other's throats over what one of them called "broken promises." Discussion revealed that words one had interpreted as a firm commitment were merely aspirational to his counterpart.

Sometimes even laudable organizational goals can engender troublesome communication dynamics: For example, corporations that promote a culture of positivity may end up with employees who are reluctant or afraid to challenge or criticize. As the marketing director of a fast-moving consumer goods firm told us: "You're not supposed to be negative about people's ideas. What's going through the back of your mind is 'I can't see this working.' But what comes out of your mouth is 'Yeah, that's great.'"

When teams discuss at the outset how much candor is appropriate, they can establish clear guidelines about speaking up or pushing back on others. At a German investment bank, a top team that had been dominated by several assertive consultants adopted a "four sentence" rule—a cutoff for each person's contributions in meetings—as a way to encourage taking turns and give more-reserved members a chance to contribute. At Heineken USA, board members use little toy horses that sit on the conference table to accomplish the same goal: If you're talking and someone tips one over, you know you're beating a dead horse and it's time to move on.

Think: Occupying Different Mindsets

Perhaps the biggest source of conflict on teams stems from the way in which members think about the work they're doing. Their varied personalities and experiences make them alert to varying signals and cause them to take different approaches to problem solving and decision making. This can result in their working at cross-purposes. As one executive with a U.S. apparel company noted: "There is often tension between the ready-fire-aim types on our team and the more analytical colleagues."

We found this dynamic in a new-product team at a Dutch consumer goods company. Members' cognitive styles differed greatly, particularly with regard to methodical versus intuitive thinking. Once aware of the problem, the project manager initiated discussions about ways to rotate leadership of the project, matching team needs to mindsets. During the more creative and conceptual phases, the freethinkers would be in charge, while analytical and detail-oriented members would take over evaluation, organization, and implementation activities. All members came to understand the value of the different approaches.

Think: Questions to Ask

In your world:

- Is uncertainty viewed as a threat or an opportunity?
- What's more important: the big picture or the details?
- Is it better to be reliable or flexible?
- What is the attitude toward failure?
- How do people tolerate deviations from the plan?

Teams also need to find alignment on tolerance for risk and shifting priorities. A striking example comes from a biotech team made up of scientists and executives. By virtue of their training, the scientists embraced experimentation, accepted failure as part of the discovery process, and valued the continued pursuit of breakthroughs, regardless of time horizon or potential for commercial applications. That mindset jarred their MBA-trained peers, who sought predictability in results and preferred to kill projects that failed to meet expectations. To bridge those differences, a facilitator used role play to help the two groups better understand each other's perspective.

Feel: Charting Emotionals

Team members may differ widely in the intensity of their feelings, how they convey passion in a group, and the way they manage their emotions in the face of disagreement or conflict.

Sometimes enthusiasm can overwhelm peers or fuel skepticism. An extroverted CMO at a logistics company we worked with assumed that the more passion she showed for her ideas, the more responsive the group would be to them. But her "rah-rah" approach was too much for the introverted, pragmatic CEO. She would start picking apart proposals whenever the CMO got excited. At the other extreme, strong negative emotions—especially overt displays of anger—can be upsetting or intimidating.

Negative feelings can be a sensitive issue to broach, so it's helpful to start by talking about the kind of context team members are used

Feel: Questions to Ask

In your world:

- What emotions (positive and negative) are acceptable and unacceptable to display in a business context?
- How do people express anger or enthusiasm?
- How would you react if you were annoyed with a teammate (with silence, body language, humor, through a third party)?

---

to. From there, the discussion can get more personal. For example, in one conversation we facilitated at a construction company, an executive told his colleagues that "yelling was common" in his previous workplace—but that it was a habit he wanted to correct. He told us that he had made this disclosure to "keep [him]self honest" in pursuit of that goal.

Early discussions should touch on not only the risks of venting but also the danger of bottling things up. The tendency to signal irritation or discontent indirectly—through withdrawal, sarcasm, and privately complaining about one another—can be just as destructive as volatile outbursts and intimidation. It's important to address the causes of disengagement directly, through open inquiry and debate, and come up with ways to disagree productively.

The benefits of anticipating and heading off conflict before it becomes destructive are immense. We've found that they include greater participation, improved creativity, and, ultimately, smarter decision making. As one manager put it: "We still disagree, but there's less bad blood and a genuine sense of valuing each other's contributions."

Originally published in June 2016. Reprint R1606F

Getting to *Sí, Ja, Oui, Hai,* and *Da*

by Erin Meyer

TIM CARR, AN AMERICAN working for a defense company based in the midwestern United States, was about to enter a sensitive bargaining session with a high-level Saudi Arabian customer, but he wasn't particularly concerned. Carr was an experienced negotiator and was well-trained in basic principles: Separate the people from the problem. Define your BATNA (best alternative to a negotiated agreement) up front. Focus on interests, not positions. He'd been there, read that, and done the training.

The lengthy phone call to Saudi Arabia proceeded according to plan. Carr carefully steered the would-be customer to accept the deal, and it seemed he had reached his goal. "So let me just review," he said. "You've agreed that you will provide the supplies for next year's project and contact your counterpart at the energy office to get his approval. I will then send a letter. . . . Next you've said that you will. . . ." But when Carr finished his detailed description of who had agreed to what, he was greeted with silence. Finally a soft but firm voice said, "I told you I would do it. You think I don't keep my promises? That I'm not good on my word?"

That was the end of the discussion—and of the deal.

The many theories about negotiation may work perfectly when you're doing a deal with a company in your own country. But in today's globalized economy you could be negotiating a joint venture in China, an outsourcing agreement in India, or a supplier contract in Sweden. If so, you might find yourself working with very different norms of communication. What gets you to "yes" in one culture gets you to "no" in another. To be effective, a negotiator must have a sense of how his counterpart is reacting. Does she want to cooperate? Is she eager, frustrated, doubtful? If you take stock of subtle messages, you can adjust your own behavior accordingly. In an international negotiation, however, you may not have the contextual understanding to interpret your counterpart's communication—especially unspoken signals—accurately. In my work and research, I find that when managers from different parts of the world negotiate, they frequently misread such signals, reach erroneous conclusions, and act, as Tim Carr did, in ways that thwart their ultimate goals.

In the following pages, I draw on my work on cross-cultural management to identify five rules of thumb for negotiating with someone whose cultural style of communication differs from yours. The trick, as we will see, is to be aware of key negotiation signals and to adjust both your perceptions and your actions in order to get the best results.

1. Adapt the Way You Express Disagreement

In some cultures it's appropriate to say "I totally disagree" or to tell the other party he's wrong. This is seen as part of a normal, healthy discussion. A Russian student of mine told me, "In Russia we enter the negotiation ready for a great big debate. If your Russian counterpart tells you passionately that he completely disagrees with every point you have made, it's not a sign that things are starting poorly. On the contrary, it's an invitation to a lively discussion."

In other cultures the same behavior would provoke anger and possibly an irreconcilable breakdown of the relationship. An American manager named Sean Green, who had spent years negotiating partnerships in Mexico, told me that he quickly learned that if he wanted to make progress toward a deal, he needed to say things like "I do not quite understand your point" and "Please explain more why you think that." If he said, "I disagree with that," the discussions might shut down completely.

Idea in Brief

The Problem

In cross-border negotiations, managers often discover that perfectly rational deals fall apart when their counterparts make what seem to be unreasonable demands or don't respect their commitments.

Why It Happens

Each culture has its own communication norms, and over time you'll find that what gets you to "yes" in one culture may get you to "no" in another.

The Solution

You can reduce miscommunication by respecting these five rules of thumb:

1. Figure out how to express disagreement.
2. Recognize what emotional expressiveness signifies.
3. Learn how the other culture builds trust.
4. Avoid yes-or-no questions.
5. Beware of putting it in writing.

The key is to listen for verbal cues—specifically, what linguistics experts call "upgraders" and "downgraders." Upgraders are words you might use to strengthen your disagreement, such as "totally," "completely," "absolutely." Downgraders—such as "partially," "a little bit," "maybe"—soften the disagreement. Russians, the French, Germans, Israelis, and the Dutch use a lot of upgraders with disagreement. Mexicans, Thai, the Japanese, Peruvians, and Ghanaians use a lot of downgraders.

Try to understand upgraders and downgraders within their own cultural context. If a Peruvian you're negotiating with says he "disagrees a little," a serious problem may well be brewing. But if your German counterpart says he "completely disagrees," you may be on the verge of a highly enjoyable debate.

2. Know When to Bottle It Up or Let It All Pour Out

In some cultures it's common—and entirely appropriate—during negotiations to raise your voice when excited, laugh passionately, touch your counterpart on the arm, or even put a friendly arm around him. In other cultures such self-expression not only feels intrusive or surprising but may even demonstrate a lack of professionalism.

121

What makes international negotiations interesting (and complicated) is that people from some very emotionally expressive cultures—such as Brazil, Mexico, and Saudi Arabia—may also avoid open disagreement. (See the exhibit "Preparing to face your counterpart.") Mexicans tend to disagree softly yet express emotions openly. As a Mexican manager, Pedro Alvarez, says, "In Mexico we perceive emotional expressiveness as a sign of honesty. Yet we are highly sensitive to negative comments and offended easily. If you disagree with me too strongly, I would read that as a signal that you don't like me."

In other cultures—such as Denmark, Germany, and the Netherlands—open disagreement is seen as positive as long as

Preparing to face your counterpart

The map below sorts nationalities according to how confrontational and emotionally expressive they are. Although negotiators often believe that the two characteristics go hand in hand, that's not always the case.

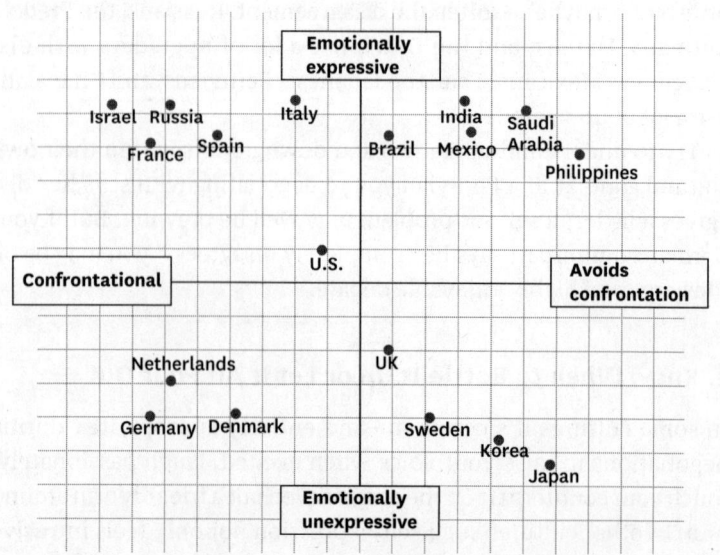

it is expressed calmly and factually. A German negotiator, Dirk Firnhaber, explains that the German word *Sachlichkeit,* most closely translated in English as "objectivity," refers to separating opinions from the person expressing them. If he says, "I totally disagree," he means to debate the opinions, not disapprove of the individual.

People from cultures like these may view emotional expressiveness as a lack of maturity or professionalism in a business context. Firnhaber tells a story about one deal he negotiated with a French company. It began calmly enough, but as the discussion continued, the French managers grew animated: "The more we discussed, the more our French colleagues became emotional—with voices raised, arms waving, ears turning red . . . the whole thing." Firnhaber was increasingly uncomfortable with the conversation and at times thought the deal would fall apart. To his surprise, the French took a very different view: "When the discussion was over, they seemed delighted with the meeting, and we all went out for a great dinner."

So the second rule of international negotiations is to recognize what an emotional outpouring (whether yours or theirs) signifies in the culture you are negotiating with, and to adapt your reaction accordingly. Was it a bad sign that the Swedish negotiators sat calmly across the table from you, never entered into open debate, and showed little passion during the discussion? Not at all. But if you encountered the same behavior while negotiating in Israel, it might be a sign that the deal was about to die an early death.

3. Learn How the Other Culture Builds Trust

During a negotiation, both parties are explicitly considering whether the deal will benefit their own business and implicitly trying to assess whether they can trust each other. Here cultural differences hit us hard. How we come to trust someone varies dramatically from one part of the world to another.

Consider this story from John Katz, an Australian negotiating a joint venture in China. Initially, he felt he was struggling to get the information his side needed, so he asked his company's China consultant for advice. The consultant suggested that Katz was going at the deal too quickly and should spend more time building trust. When Katz said he'd been working hard to do just that by supplying a lot of information from his side and answering all questions transparently, the consultant replied, "The problem is that you need to approach them from a relationship perspective, not a business perspective. You won't get what you want unless you develop trust differently."

Research in this area divides trust into two categories: *cognitive* and *affective*. Cognitive trust is based on the confidence you feel in someone's accomplishments, skills, and reliability. This trust comes from the head. In a negotiation it builds through the business interaction: You know your stuff. You are reliable, pleasant, and consistent. You demonstrate that your product or service is of high quality. I trust you. Affective trust arises from feelings of emotional closeness, empathy, or friendship. It comes from the heart. We laugh together, relax together, and see each other on a personal level, so I feel affection or empathy for you. I trust you.

In a business setting, the dominant type of trust varies dramatically from one part of the world to another. In one research project, Professor Roy Chua, of Singapore Management University, surveyed Chinese and American executives from a wide range of industries, asking them to list up to 24 important members of their professional networks. He then asked them to indicate the extent to which they felt comfortable sharing their personal problems and dreams with each of those contacts. "These items showed an affective-based willingness to depend on and be vulnerable to the other person," Chua explains. Finally, participants were asked to indicate how reliable, competent, and knowledgeable each contact was. These assessments showed a more cognitive-based willingness to depend on the other person.

The survey revealed that in negotiations (and business in general) Americans draw a sharp line between cognitive and affective trust. American culture has a long tradition of separating the emotional from the practical. Mixing the two risks conflict of interest and is viewed as unprofessional. Chinese managers, however, connect the two, and the interplay between cognitive and affective trust is much stronger. They are quite likely to develop personal bonds where they have financial or business ties.

In most emerging or newly emerged markets, from BRIC to Southeast Asia and Africa, negotiators are unlikely to trust their counterparts until an affective connection has been made. The same is true for most Middle Eastern and Mediterranean cultures. That may make negotiations challenging for task-oriented Americans, Australians, Brits, or Germans. Ricardo Bartolome, a Spanish manager, told me that he finds Americans to be very friendly on the surface, sometimes surprisingly so, but difficult to get to know at a deeper level. "During a negotiation they are so politically correct and careful not to show negative emotion," he said. "It makes it hard for us to trust them."

So in certain cultures you need to build an affective bond or emotional connection as early as possible. Invest time in meals and drinks (or tea, karaoke, golf, whatever it may be), and don't talk about the deal during these activities. Let your guard down and show your human side, including your weaknesses. Demonstrate genuine interest in the other party and make a friend. Be patient: In China, for example, this type of bond may take a long time to build. Eventually, you won't have just a friend; you'll have a deal.

4. Avoid Yes-or-No Questions

At some point during your negotiation you'll need to put a proposal on the table—and at that moment you will expect to hear whether or not the other side accepts. One of the most confounding aspects of international negotiations is that in some cultures the word "yes" may be used when the real meaning is no. In other cultures "no" is the most frequent knee-jerk response, but it often means "Let's discuss further." In either case, misunderstanding the message can lead to a waste of time or a muddled setback.

A recent negotiation between a Danish company and its Indonesian supplier provides a case in point. One of the Danish executives wanted reassurance that the Indonesians could meet the desired deadline, so he asked them directly if the date was feasible.

Look for Cultural Bridges

THERE'S NO SUBSTITUTE for learning all you can about the culture you will be negotiating with. But taking a cultural bridge—someone who is from the other culture, has a foot in both cultures, or, at the very least, knows the other culture intimately—to the negotiating table will give you a head start.

Of course, if one party doesn't speak English well, it's common to have the help of a translator; but a cultural bridge can make a huge impact even if no linguistic divide exists. During breaks in the negotiation, for example, you can ask this person to interpret what's going on between the lines.

The British executive Sarah Stevens was leading a U.S. team negotiating a deal in Japan. The Japanese parties all spoke English well, but three hours into the negotiation Stevens realized that her team was doing 90% of the talking, which worried her. She asked a colleague from her company's Japan office for advice. He explained that the Japanese often pause to think before speaking—and that they don't find silence uncomfortable the way Americans or the British do. He advised Stevens to adopt the Japanese approach: After asking a question, wait patiently and quietly for an answer. He also told her that the Japanese often make decisions in groups, so they might need to confer before giving an answer. If after a period of silence no clear answer had been given, Stevens might suggest a short break so that they could have a sidebar.

To his face they replied that it was, but a few days later they informed the company by e-mail that it was not. The Danish executive was aggrieved. "We'd already wasted weeks," he says. "Why didn't they tell us transparently during the meeting? We felt they had lied to us point-blank."

After hearing this story, I asked an Indonesian manager to explain what had happened. He told me that from an Indonesian perspective, it is rude to look someone you respect and like in the eye and say no to a request. "Instead we try to show 'no' with our body language or voice tone," he said. "Or perhaps we say, 'We will try our best.'" Signals like these are a way of saying "We would like to do what you want, but it is not possible." The interlocutor assumes that his counterpart will get the message and that both parties can then move on.

The problem can work the other way. The Indonesian manager went on to describe his experience negotiating with a French

In Japan, he said, it is common to iron out a lot of potential conflicts in one-on-one informal discussions before the formal group meeting, which is seen more as a place to put a stamp on decisions already made. This particular nugget came too late for that trip, but Stevens made sure the next time to enable informal discussions in advance. Thanks to her cultural bridge, she got the deal she had hoped for.

If your team has no obvious candidate for this role, look elsewhere in your company. But don't make the common mistake of thinking that someone who speaks the language and has a parent from the culture will necessarily make a good cultural bridge.

Consider this British manager of Korean origin: He looked Korean, had a Korean name, and spoke Korean with no accent, but he'd never lived or worked in Korea; his parents had moved to Britain as teenagers. His company asked him to help with an important negotiation in Korea, but once there, he quickly realized that his team would have been better off without him. Because he spoke the language so well, the Koreans assumed that he would behave like a Korean, so they took offense when he spoke to the wrong person in the room and when he confronted them too directly. As he observes, "If I hadn't looked or sounded Korean, they would have forgiven me for behaving badly."

company for the first time: "When I asked them if they could kindly do something, the word 'no' flew out of their mouths—and not just once but often more like a 'no-no-no-no,' which feels to us like we are being slapped repeatedly." He found out later that the French were actually happy to accede to his request; they had just wanted to debate it a bit before final agreement.

When you need to know whether your counterpart is willing to do something, but his answer to every question leaves you more confused than before, remember the fourth rule of cross-cultural negotiations: If possible, avoid posing a yes-or-no question. Rather than "Will you do this?" try "How long would it take you to get this done?" And when you do ask a yes-or-no question in Southeast Asia, Japan, or Korea (perhaps also in India or Latin America), engage all your senses and emotional antennae. Even if the response is affirmative, something may feel like no: an extra beat of silence, a strong sucking in of the breath, a muttered "I will try, but it will be difficult." If so, the deal is probably not sealed. You may well have more negotiations in front of you.

5. Be Careful About Putting It in Writing

American managers learn early on to repeat key messages frequently and recap a meeting in writing. "Tell them what you're going to tell them, tell them, and then tell them what you've told them" is one of the first communication lessons taught in the United States. In Northern Europe, too, clarity and repetition are the basis of effective negotiation.

But this good practice can all too often sour during negotiations in Africa or Asia. A woman from Burundi who was working for a Dutch company says, "In my culture, if we have a discussion on the phone and come to a verbal agreement, that would be enough for me. If you get off the phone and send me a written recap of the discussion, that would be a clear signal that you don't trust me." This, she says, repeatedly caused difficulty for her company's negotiators, who recapped each discussion in writing as a matter of both habit and principle.

The difference in approach can make it difficult to write a contract. Americans rely heavily on written contracts—more so than any other culture in the world. As soon as two parties have agreed on the price and details, long documents outlining what will happen if the deal is not kept, and requiring signatures, are exchanged. In the U.S. these contracts are legally binding and make it easy to do business with people we otherwise have no reason to trust.

But in countries where the legal system is traditionally less reliable, and relationships carry more weight in business, written contracts are less frequent. In these countries they are often a commitment to do business but may not be legally binding. Therefore they're less detailed and less important. As one Nigerian manager explains, "If the moment we come to an agreement, you pull out the contract and hand me a pen, I start to worry. Do you think I won't follow through? Are you trying to trap me?"

In Nigeria and many other high-growth markets where the business environment is rapidly evolving, such as China and Indonesia, successful businesspeople must be much more flexible than is necessary (or desirable) in the West. In these cultures, a contract marks the beginning of a relationship, but it is understood that as the situation changes, the details of the agreement will also change.

Consider the experience of John Wagner, an American who had been working out a deal with a Chinese supplier. After several days of tough negotiations, his team and its legal department drafted a contract that the Chinese seemed happy to sign. But about six weeks later they reopened discussion on points that the Americans thought had been set in stone. Wagner observes, "I see now that we appeared irrationally inflexible to them. But at the time, we were hitting our heads against our desks." For the Americans, the contract had closed the negotiation phase, and implementation would follow. But for the Chinese, signing the contract was just one step in the dance.

So the fifth and final rule for negotiating internationally is to proceed cautiously with the contract. Ask your counterparts to draft the first version so that you can discern how much detail they are planning to commit to before you plunk down a 20-page document for them to sign. And be ready to revisit. When negotiating in emerging markets, remember that everything in these countries is dynamic, and no deal is ever really 100% final.

———

Finally, don't forget the universal rules: When you are negotiating a deal, you need to persuade and react, to convince and finesse, pushing your points while working carefully toward an agreement. In the heat of the discussion, what is spoken is important. But the trust you have built, the subtle messages you have understood, your ability to adapt your demeanor to the context at hand, will ultimately make the difference between success and failure—for Americans, for Chinese, for Brazilians, for everybody.

Originally published in December 2015. Reprint R1512E

Cultivating Everyday Courage

by James R. Detert

IN MANY STORIES we hear about workplace courage, the people who fight for positive change end up being ostracized—and sometimes even lose their jobs. What I've seen in the course of my research, though, tells a more nuanced story. Most acts of courage don't come from whistleblowers or organizational martyrs. Instead, they come from respected insiders at all levels who take action— be it campaigning for a risky strategic move, pushing to change an unfair policy, or speaking out against unethical behavior—because they believe it's the right thing to do. Their reputations and track records enable them to make more headway than those on the margins or outside the organization could. And when they manage the process well, they don't necessarily pay a high price for their actions; indeed, they may see their status rise as they create positive change.

Consider Martha (not her real name), a finance manager at a small company. For years she endured risqué comments and sexual innuendo from her boss, the company president, and she struggled with how to handle it: Should she talk to him about his behavior, or just quit? How could she protect the other women at the firm? Then, at a staff gathering, her boss grabbed her inappropriately during a light moment, thinking it was funny. Later that day, she confronted him in his office, prepared to quit if he made no changes. She told him that his behavior made her uncomfortable and was a signal to her that she'd never advance in the company because he didn't view her as an equal. She said that perhaps he was trying to promote a fun work environment, but he was failing.

Martha was terrified that he would fire her, be angry, or tell her to toughen up. But instead, to her surprise, he apologized. He was horrified that this was how she felt—and that other women in the company probably felt the same way. He praised her for speaking out when no one else had dared to. Over subsequent months, he continued to seek her guidance on the issue and made a formal apology to the staff. A year later, Martha was promoted to a VP role: an incredible position to be in for someone who once believed that the president would never promote a woman to that level.

I began investigating workplace courage after spending more than a decade studying why people so often don't speak up at work. I've found many examples of people at all levels who created positive change without ruining their careers. Their success rested primarily on a set of attitudes and behaviors that can be learned, rather than on innate characteristics. I call people who exhibit these behaviors *competently courageous* because they create the right conditions for action by establishing a strong internal reputation and by improving their fallback options in case things go poorly; they carefully choose their battles, discerning whether a given opportunity to act makes sense in light of their values, the timing, and their broader objectives; they maximize the odds of in-the-moment success by managing the messaging and emotions; and they follow up to preserve relationships and marshal commitment. These steps are useful whether you're pushing for major change or trying to address a smaller or more local issue.

Lest anyone think I'm naive, let me be clear: Of course bad things do happen when people challenge authorities, norms, and institutions. Courage, after all, is about taking worthy actions *despite the potential risk*. If no one ever got fired, was socially isolated, or suffered other consequences for a particular action, we wouldn't consider it courageous. And good outcomes are more likely to

Idea in Brief

The Challenge

Professionals who perform courageous acts—such as pushing to change a flawed policy or speaking out against unethical behavior—risk their reputations and even their jobs.

A Better Way

People who succeed in their courageous acts, or suffer fewer negative consequences, tend to exhibit certain behaviors and attributes: They lay the groundwork for action; they carefully choose their battles; they manage messaging and emotions; and they follow up afterward.

Getting Started

A good way to learn and master competently courageous behaviors is to engage in smaller, everyday acts before proceeding to progressively more difficult ones. Above all, keep your values and purpose front and center.

come from some types of actions than from others. For example, challenging the inappropriate behavior of a colleague with whom you have a decent relationship is, all else being equal, likely to go better for you than defying the entire power structure over an unethical practice.

Among those I studied who had failed to create positive change, almost all still thought their risk-taking had been the right thing to do. They were proud they had stood up for what they believed in—but they wished they'd done so more skillfully. Following the four principles laid out here can help people at all levels improve their chances of creating positive change when they do decide to act.

Laying the Groundwork

My research shows that employees whose workplace courage produces good results have often spent months or years establishing that they excel at their jobs, that they are invested in the organization, and that they're evenhanded. They've demonstrated that they're able to stand both apart from and with those whose support they need. In doing so, they've accumulated what psychologists call idiosyncrasy credits—a stock of goodwill derived from their history of competence and conformity—which they can cash in when challenging norms or those with more power. (I've also seen the reverse: When people with a reputation for selfishness or ill will stand up for legitimately needed change, they tend to be less successful.)

Competently courageous people also work to earn the trust of those who see them as their champions. They invest in those relationships, too—engaging with people individually, taking the time to empathize with them, and helping them develop professionally.

Consider Catherine Gill, a former senior vice president of fundraising and communication at the nonprofit social investment fund Root Capital. Gill wanted to speak up about what she and colleagues saw as the organization's unintentional yet manifest internal bias against women. The issue was particularly tricky because criticizing the leadership could easily be viewed as criticizing the organization's socially conscious mission. But she was able to launch an honest—if painful—conversation with her colleagues in senior management about the organization's culture, leading to a number of concrete changes.

Gill's track record of excelling and fitting in at the organization was fundamental to her success. Over her first two years at Root Capital, she achieved consistently high performance as a fundraiser and exhibited the emotional and intellectual intelligence to navigate complex issues. She showed that she was deeply committed to the organization's mission, regularly adjusting her role to tackle the most pressing challenges and showing how various initiatives she launched were aligned with core strategic priorities. She was careful to point out when she didn't consider something a gender issue so that people on both sides would see her as fair. All that gave her the idiosyncrasy credits she needed to be heard by the leadership team. She determined the limits of what change was possible so that she wouldn't push too far and get "voted off the island." Through her work ethic, judgment, and humor, she set the stage for more visible moments of courageous action.

Sometimes things don't work out, even with the best preparation. Competently courageous people develop mechanisms to mitigate fallout. That might mean finding ways to make themselves indispensable to the organization, keeping external options open, or minimizing economic reliance on an employer. For example, former Telecom Italia leader Franco Bernabè rejected many of the perks that came with being the CEO of a major company, knowing that doing so made it easier to take risks. "If I had lost my job," he said, "and gone back to something more subdued and less glamorous—well, it wouldn't have changed my life."

Choosing Your Battles

Not every opportunity to display courage is worth taking. The people I've studied who have been successful in their courageous acts asked themselves two questions before moving ahead: Is this really important? and, Is this the right time?

Importance, of course, lies in the eye of the beholder. It depends on your goals and values and those of your colleagues, stakeholders, and the organization itself. As you gauge whether an issue is truly important, be aware of your emotional triggers; allow yourself to be informed but not held hostage by them. Also assess whether engaging in a potential battle—whatever the outcome might be—is likely to aid or hinder winning the war. Ask yourself, for example: Will securing resources to address this problem make it less likely that a higher-priority proposal will subsequently get funded?

Competently courageous people are masters of good timing. To avoid being seen as a broken record, they are less likely to act if they recently cashed in hard-earned idiosyncrasy credits. They observe what is going on around them, and if the timing doesn't look right, they patiently hold off. They scan the environment for events and trends that could support their efforts, making the most of an organizational change or the appearance of a new ally, for example. They stay attuned to attention cycles—to public upwellings of enthusiasm for the issue at hand. Pushing for a more globally representative strategy or leadership team, for example, was for a long time risky in many organizations; now companies are more open to tackling those issues. Unless they've concluded that taking action is necessary to preserve their sense of integrity or to plant the seed of an idea, competently courageous people don't act before those around them are ready to take them seriously.

For example, when "Mandy" joined an accessories and apparel company as a product manager, she quickly learned that one of the company's vendors was highly problematic. Its reps were rude, dishonest, and manipulative, and the product itself was subpar. However, ties between the two companies were long-standing and included a friendship between two key managers. Mandy wisely waited; she didn't suggest a change until six months later. By that point she had demonstrated her commitment to the organization, and she was better able to gauge the relationships between the people involved. She used the intervening time to collect evidence of the problems, identify alternative vendors, and quantify the improvements they could offer. When she finally did make her proposal, the VP in charge responded positively.

In some cases, conditions or events such as sagging sales or a change in leadership create urgency for courageous acts—and make them more likely to succeed. Tachi Yamada, a physician-scientist turned business leader, has been a master of seizing the day during a successful career as a senior executive in the health care sector. When Yamada became head of R&D at Smith Kline Beecham in 1999, he quickly concluded that the R&D organization needed to be restructured around disease areas or "assets" (the molecules or compounds that might eventually make it to market) rather than the traditional silos. When a merger with another pharmaceutical giant—Glaxo—was announced, he campaigned for the R&D function of the combined company to be structured in that way. The proposal didn't go over well. R&D leaders and scientists at Glaxo were particularly upset; here was the new guy from the much smaller company in the merger telling them they needed a major change. They "were pretty much aligned against me," recalls Yamada. But he knew that the timing could be used to

Further Reading

"Get the Boss to Buy In," by Susan J. Ashford and James R. Detert (HBR, January–February 2015)

"Harnessing the Science of Persuasion," by Robert B. Cialdini (HBR, October 2001)

"Conducting Difficult Conversations," by Karen Dillon in *HBR Guide to Office Politics* (HBR Press, 2014)

"The Necessary Art of Persuasion," by Jay A. Conger (HBR, May–June 1998)

"Moves That Matter: Issue Selling and Organizational Change," by Jane E. Dutton, Susan J. Ashford, Regina M. O'Neill, and Katherine A. Lawrence (*Academy of Management Journal*, 2001)

Giving Voice to Values: How to Speak Your Mind When You Know What's Right, by Mary C. Gentile (Yale University Press, 2012)

Made to Stick: Why Some Ideas Survive and Others Die, by Chip Heath and Dan Heath (Random House, 2007)

his advantage: "The merger and the thin pipeline in both companies gave me a burning platform." His push for the reorganization succeeded in part because of his ability to recognize the opportunity and capitalize on it.

Persuading in the Moment

Workplace courage is, of course, about more than preparation. Eventually you must take action. During this step, competently courageous people focus primarily on three things: framing their issue in terms that the audience will relate to, making effective use of data, and managing the emotions in the room. (See "Further Reading" for more on persuasion.) They connect their agenda to the organization's priorities or values, or explain how it addresses critical areas of concern for stakeholders. They ensure that decision makers feel included—not attacked or pushed aside.

Mel Exon, a former executive at the advertising firm Bartle Bogle Hegarty (BBH), excels at framing proposals in ways that make them attractive to those whose support she needs. For example, when Exon and a colleague first pitched the idea for an internal innovation unit—BBH Labs—to senior management, support was far from unanimous. Some executives worried that the creation of a separate innovation group would imply that parts of BBH *weren't* innovative. This was concerning in a firm that proudly considered itself the contrarian visionary in the industry, with a black sheep as its calling card.

To convince the skeptics that BBH Labs was philosophically aligned with the company's mission, Exon took advantage of internal stakeholders' pride in the black sheep image, pointing out that some of BBH's clients had come to the company specifically for groundbreaking ideas. A lab focused on innovation would fulfill exactly that need. She won over others by describing the work of the new lab as advance scouting, promising that everyone at the firm would share in its findings. Exon eventually got the go-ahead from senior management, and later BBH's CEO complimented her approach, describing it as building on the company's DNA rather than trying to change it.

Keeping your cool as you perform your courageous act can be just as important as how you make your case. A manager I'll call Erik, who was tasked with growing the solar business at one of the world's largest multinationals, frequently butted heads with senior executives in the company's traditional lines of business. When he sought their support for new business models, they often pushed back, telling him brusquely, "We don't do that" or "That will never work here." The discussions could get heated, and Erik often felt frustrated by the executives' defensiveness. But instead of taking the emotional bait, he reminded himself that their response was a normal reaction to fear of the unknown. Acknowledging their mindset helped him stay calm and concentrate on simply making data-driven arguments. In the end, he was able to bring others around to his point of view, and the business made a strong pivot toward his recommended strategy.

Following Up

Those who exhibit competent courage follow up after they take action, no matter how things turned out. They manage their relationships with the people involved: When things go well, they thank supporters and share credit. When things go badly, they address lingering emotions and repair ties with those who might be hurt or angry.

For example, Catherine Gill made an in-the-moment decision to launch her campaign to change the culture at Root Capital during a retreat with about 30 leaders present. But as a result of her spontaneous decision, she caught the CEO off guard. Knowing that the very difficult conversation that ensued might have felt to him like an indictment of his leadership—and that he might see her actions as a personal attack—Gill checked in with him privately at that evening's dinner. She assured him that she wasn't trying to start a revolution; she was trying to advance the firm's evolution into its ideal form.

Follow-up also means continuing to pursue your agenda beyond the first big moment of action. Even when their initial steps go well, the competently courageous continue to advocate, reach out to secure resources, and make sure others deliver on promises. And when things don't go well, they take it in stride, viewing setbacks as learning opportunities rather than hiding from the fallout or giving up.

Take Fred Keller, who established a welfare-to-career program at the company he founded, Cascade Engineering. In the initiative's first incarnation, participants were often late or absent, and their performance was poor. Within a few weeks, not one of the new hires remained, and Cascade's employees and supervisors were left feeling frustrated. Instead of giving up, Keller viewed the failure as an opportunity to learn. Finding that neither Cascade nor its new hires had been well prepared for the program, he reinstated it with more training for everyone involved. When this second attempt seemed headed toward a similar fate, Keller harnessed the growing criticism to get it right. He further increased training of leaders and partnered with a county official to bring a social worker on-site to work with the new hires to identify and solve problems before they escalated.

This time Keller's persistence and learning paid off: The program is now a core part of the organization and is widely lauded as a model for transitioning people from welfare to work. And through his persistence, Keller earned tremendous loyalty from his staff at all levels of the company.

Getting Started

Courage isn't required only for high-stakes campaigns. My research with Evan Bruno, a PhD student at Darden, shows that a host of everyday actions require employees to act courageously. Sometimes simply doing one's job well requires courage. It's also worth noting that "risk" encompasses more than the prospect of financial ruin or getting fired. Humans naturally fear rejection, embarrassment, and all sorts of other social and economic consequences. From the outside, for example, it might be easy to question whether Fred Keller's actions required courage. As the owner of the company, Keller could do whatever he wanted, so where's the risk? But for years, he faced doubters both inside and outside his organization. To persevere knowing that people might think he was a "nutcase" or that he was wasting time or money took courage.

The good news is that the experiences of those I've studied show that competently courageous behaviors can be learned. They're dependent on effort and practice, rather than on some heroic personality trait limited to the few. (So don't use that as an excuse to let yourself off the hook if you find yourself in a situation that calls for courage!) One piece of advice I give to students and clients: Don't jump into the deep end right away. Instead, approach this work incrementally by trying smaller, more manageable acts before proceeding to progressively harder ones. That might mean having a difficult conversation in some other sphere of life, or broaching a tough topic with a colleague you like and respect, before confronting a boss about demeaning behavior. It might mean guiding your own team in a new direction before suggesting a transformation of the whole organization. And consider what "small" means to you—we all have different perceptions of which actions require courage. (To see how your perception of what takes courage lines up with others', take our Workplace Courage Acts Index self-assessment at www .workplacecai.com.) Then, as you tackle each step, focus on what you learn, not whether it goes perfectly the first time.

Above all, keep your values and purpose front and center. You'll have a stronger sense of self-respect through any setbacks you face, and you'll be less likely to regret your actions, no matter how things turn out. And by using the principles discussed in this article, you'll increase the chances of successfully creating change, making the risks you take all the more worthwhile.

Originally published in November–December 2018. Reprint R1806K

Research & Development at the NeuroLeadership Institute

About the Contributors

JEAN-LOUIS BARSOUX is a term research professor at IMD.

SCOTT BERINATO is a senior editor at Harvard Business Review and the author of *Good Charts Workbook: Tips, Tools, and Exercises for Making Better Data Visualizations* and *Good Charts: The HBR Guide to Making Smarter, More Persuasive Data Visualizations.*

ALISON WOOD BROOKS is the O'Brien Associate Professor of Business Administration at Harvard Business School.

JAMES R. DETERT is a professor of business administration and the associate dean of Executive Degree Programs and Leadership Initiatives at the University of Virginia's Darden School of Business.

DAVID A. GARVIN was the C. Roland Christensen Professor at Harvard Business School.

HEIDI GRANT is a social psychologist who researches, writes, and speaks about the science of motivation. She is Global Director of Research & Development at the NeuroLeadership Institute and serves as Associate Director of Columbia's Motivation Science Center. She received her doctorate in social psychology from Columbia University. Her most recent book is *Reinforcements: How to Get People to Help You.* She's also the author of *Nine Things Successful People Do Differently* and *No One Understands You and What to Do About It.*

BORIS GROYSBERG is the Richard P. Chapman Professor of Business Administration at Harvard Business School, Faculty Affiliate at the HBS Gender Initiative, and the coauthor, with Michael Slind, of *Talk, Inc.* (Harvard Business Review Press, 2012).

SHEILA HEEN teaches negotiation at Harvard Law School and is a principal at Triad Consulting Group. She is a coauthor of the *New York Times* bestsellers *Thanks for the Feedback* (Viking/Penguin, 2014) with Douglas Stone and *Difficult Conversations* with Douglas Stone and Bruce Patton.

LESLIE K. JOHN is an associate professor of business administration at Harvard Business School.

PAUL LEONARDI is the Duca Family Professor of Technology Management at the University of California, Santa Barbara, and advises companies about how to use social network data and new technologies to improve performance and employee well-being.

JOSHUA D. MARGOLIS is the James Dinan and Elizabeth Miller Professor of Business Administration and the head of the Organizational Behavior unit at Harvard Business School.

ERIN MEYER is a professor at INSEAD, where she directs the executive education program Leading Across Borders and Cultures. She is the author of *The Culture Map: Breaking Through the Invisible Boundaries of Global Business* (PublicAffairs, 2014).

TSEDAL NEELEY is the Naylor Fitzhugh Professor of Business Administration in the Organizational Behavior Unit at Harvard Business School and the founder of the consulting firm Global Matters. She is the author of *The Language of Global Success*.

LYNN OFFERMANN is a professor of organizational sciences and communication at the George Washington University.

LISA ROSH is an assistant professor of management at the Sy Syms School of Business at Yeshiva University.

MICHAEL SLIND is a writer, editor, and communication consultant. He is coauthor of *Talk, Inc.* (Harvard Business Review Press, 2012).

DOUGLAS STONE cofounded the Triad Consulting Group and teaches negotiation at Harvard Law School. He is coauthor of the book *Thanks for the Feedback* (Viking/Penguin, 2014).

GINKA TOEGEL is a professor of organizational behavior and leadership at IMD in Lausanne, Switzerland.

Index

An all-in-one resource for every working parent.

If you enjoyed this book and want more guidance on working parenthood, turn to *Workparent: The Complete Guide to Succeeding on the Job, Staying True to Yourself, and Raising Happy Kids*. Written by Daisy Dowling, a top executive coach, talent expert, and working mom, *Workparent* provides all the advice and assurance you'll need to combine children and career In your own, authentic way.

AVAILABLE IN PAPERBACK
OR EBOOK FORMAT.

The most important management ideas all in one place.

We hope you enjoyed this book from *Harvard Business Review*. Now you can get even more with HBR's 10 Must Reads Boxed Set. From books on leadership and strategy to managing yourself and others, this 6-book collection delivers articles on the most essential business topics to help you succeed.

HBR's 10 Must Reads Series

The definitive collection of ideas and best practices on our most sought-after topics from the best minds in business.

- Change Management
- Collaboration
- Communication
- Emotional Intelligence
- Innovation
- Leadership
- Making Smart Decisions

- Managing Across Cultures
- Managing People
- Managing Yourself
- Strategic Marketing
- Strategy
- Teams
- The Essentials

hbr.org/mustreads